Daniel Augustus Drown

Idyls of Strawberry Bank

Poems

Daniel Augustus Drown

Idyls of Strawberry Bank
Poems

ISBN/EAN: 9783337004989

Printed in Europe, USA, Canada, Australia, Japan

Cover: Foto ©Thomas Meinert / pixelio.de

More available books at **www.hansebooks.com**

KIND WORDS.

THE following are extracts from testimonials and notices of Mr. Drown, and his poems, on the appearance of his first volume in 1860: —

"His position appeals to the sympathy of every generous heart. Let those who would learn how a cheerful trust can be manifested under severest trials, — how purest aspirations can arise out of intense suffering, how Christian faith can penetrate its clear vision into the eternal world, — read this book." — *R. C. W., in Boston Transcript.*

"The peoms have been written in darkness and gloom; but they are spiritually bright, and abound with beauties that the eye alone cannot see." — *Saturday Evening Gazette.*

"The pictures of life which were enjoyed and deeply imprinted in earlier years have given vivacity to the illusions of his imagination in his hours of retirement, while looking only on the half-closed volume of nature." — *Exeter News-Letter.*

"Although these poems were written under most depressing circumstances, we find in them no repining or misanthropic spirit; but, on the contrary, they breathe forth an elasticity, buoyancy, and cheerfulness of spirit, which it would seem impossible to be inspired, save by the enjoyment of a far larger share of life's blessings than falls to the lot of this young man." — *Boston Transcript.*

"The poems themselves abound in sentiment, pathos, faith, and hope. The book should have a large sale among the sons of Portsmouth for its author's sake." — *Portsmouth Chronicle.*

"For years the author has been suffering in darkness and hopelessness of cure from a painful disease of the optic nerves; but he sings like the nightingale, with a sweeter pensiveness after the red-hot iron has passed through its eyes. His poems, as might be expected, are all in the minor key; evincing a heart not hardened by his trial, and a taste and fancy vivacious and elastic under his burden." — *Christian Register.*

"We hope that, among the gifts of the season, this book will be purchased with a liberal hand; thus not only conferring a good gift on a friend, but also a needed boon to a talented and unfortunate young man, who has formed this rich bouquet of flowers, which, in his own words, 'have silently bloomed in the valley of shadow.'" — *Portsmouth Journal.*

"In his dreary confinement the muses have inspired him to utter songs whose sweet echoes invite the sympathizing without to listen and to remember the gifted author in his deep need." — *Congregational Journal.*

"The volume possesses much merit, and it is hoped will, through a generous public, prove a relief to the author's present embarrassment, and cheer in some measure whatever period of darkness may remain to him." — *Concord Statesman.*

"Made 'perfect through suffering,' his quiet life has sent forth a pure and elevating influence, which has been felt especially by those who have been personally acquainted with him, and greatly by the many who have known him only through the 'Fragrant Flowers' which he has strown for the public eye." — *Portsmouth Journal.*

PORTSMOUTH PARADE.

The self-same scene that met our boyish gaze,
Returns to greet us in the latter days,
Wherein the civil bent is manifest,
And slumberous quiet it of old possessed ;
But look upon the scene by memory's aid,
To catch the glory of the old *Parade*,
Irradiated by the flashing light
Of sacrifice on *Independence* night.

Portsmouth Revisited.

PORTSMOUTH PARADE.

IDYLS OF STRAWBERRY BANK.

POEMS:

BY

DANIEL AUGUSTUS DROWN.

"Yet I argue not
Against Heaven's hand or will, nor bate a jot
Of heart or hope; but still bear up, and steer
Right onward."

PORTSMOUTH, N.H.:
PRINTED FOR THE AUTHOR.
1873.

TO

THE SONS OF PORTSMOUTH,

MY BRETHREN,

I Dedicate my Book;

FEELING THAT,

THOUGH MY EYES NO MORE MAY SEE THEM, NOR MY HAND CLASP THEIRS IN FRIENDLY EMBRACE,

STILL

WE MAY MEET IN SPIRIT,

AND ENJOY SWEET COMMUNION THROUGH THE MEDIUM OF SONG.

"God sets some souls in shade, alone;
They have no daylight of their own:
Only in lives of happier ones
They see the shine of distant suns.

"God knows. Content thee with thy night:
The greater heaven hath grander light.
To-day is close. The hours are small:
Thou sit'st afar, and hast them all.

"Lose the less joy that doth but blind;
Reach forth a larger bliss to find.
To-day is brief: the inclusive spheres
Rain raptures of a thousand years."

TESTIMONIALS.

From Rev. A. P. Peabody, D.D.

CAMBRIDGE, Jan. 27, 1873.

MY DEAR MR. DROWN, — I am glad to learn that you are going to publish a new volume of poems. Please consider me as a subscriber, and make any use you can of my name in advancing the circulation of the book. I say this, not only because I sympathize so deeply with your sufferings, and so much admire the Christian submission, fortitude, and true heroism with which you have borne them, but because your poetry is pure, sweet, and lofty, indicating a high order of ability, delicate taste, rich imagination, and a fine command of language and rhythm.

A. P. PEABODY.

From Hon. Mellen Chamberlain.

CHELSEA, Feb. 6, 1873.

MY DEAR MR. SHILLABER, — I am glad to hear that Mr. Drown is about publishing a new volume of poems. We were college-mates, and of the class of '44. Belonging to his division, I had daily opportunity of observing him, and was early impressed with a sense of his superior scholarship and general culture. No one could have been more correct in deportment, or gentle towards all who approached him. Although he has been long withdrawn from the world, I have reason to know that his classmates still remember him with affection, and hear with admiration of the patience with which he bears his singular and long-protracted sufferings. Nor can we fail to be interested in the volume which is shortly to appear.

Very truly yours,
MELLEN CHAMBERLAIN.

The undersigned, college classmates of Mr. D. A. Drown, cheerfully bear testimony to his conscientious scholarship and amiable character while we were nearly associated with him, and cordially join in the wish that the contemplated collection of his poems — the fruits of his maturer culture, and the solace of his long years of sickness and trial — may meet with a reception from the public worthy alike of their own merits and of his blameless life and patient fortitude.

CHARLES H. BELL.
AMBROSE A. RANNEY.
EDWARD S. CUTTER.
HORATIO G. PARKER.
HARVEY JEWELL.
J. H. BRADLEY.
JOHN H. GEORGE.

FRIENDLY INTRODUCTION.

It was the privilege of the undersigned, twelve years ago, to write a preface introducing a book by Mr. Daniel A. Drown, and to call attention to certain facts relating to its author. That privilege is again exercised in a like office, — a call being made for a second volume, — and he again recounts the sorrows of his friend, asking the attention of a sympathizing public. Mr. Drown graduated at Dartmouth College in 1844, in a class composed of some of the most distinguished scholars in the country, who have made their names famous, among whom he held a respectable position. As described by one of his class-mates, — William C. Todd, Esq., — "he was one of the most correct and exemplary students in college, passing through his whole course without a stain of reproach." Graduating thus with honor, and selecting the calling of teacher, he prepared to enter upon his life-work: but, just as his arrangements were completed, he was seized with a disease of the optic nerve; and all his plans were frustrated. For five years he sought relief from the eminent oculists of our own land, but without avail. Then he was compelled to take to a darkened room; and for twenty-four years he has been shut from the light, from social companionship, from communion with nature, from all that makes life enjoyable. A sad and terrible case this; and yet, amid it all, he has found the heart to sing his songs, from a remembrance of nature, — with which he was once in sweet accord, — and a love of the true and the good, which darkness and confinement could not destroy. A strong and clear faith in God has ever sustained him. Calamity has never shaken it; and, like old Eli, he says, "It is the Lord: let him do what seemeth him good." He has found many kind friends who have ministered to him; but he shrinks from dependence: and by his book he hopes to win a return that shall place him beyond the contingency of want. The undersigned, therefore, begs the author's friends to patronize his book, from their prosperity and healthfulness, and give him the assurance, in his darkness, that they have not ceased to feel for him. He has dedicated his book to "THE SONS OF PORTSMOUTH;" and it is to be hoped that the Sons and the Daughters may respond to this affectionate tribute to his youthful friends and companions, and by their generosity relieve his mind from its dread of becoming entirely a burden. The poems are replete with goodness and beauty, simple and unaffected, and find their way to the heart through the best channels: therefore they are worthy of regard, and may be read and treasured up with benefit to the possessors, — not "Sons of Portsmouth" alone, but to all who have sympathetic hearts to feel for the poet, and taste to appreciate his rhymes.

B. P. SHILLABER.

AUTHOR'S PREFACE.

WHEN the author issued his first volume, twelve years since, he scarcely deemed that he should so long have remained to bear the physical ills he suffered, and the concomitant evil of poverty; but, for a wise purpose, undoubtedly, the good God has retained him, the most unfortunate of his children, while he has removed thousands whose lives were precious in usefulness, about whom affection clung tenaciously but vainly. His purposes none can see; but, with faith in the assurance that he doeth all things well, the heart strengthens, and the burden of life is easier borne. The author comes before his friends, and appeals to their sympathy and kindness from the depths of his long affliction, — added to by the flight of years, — and begs a passing thought which will penetrate to his retirement, and give his heart new hope. With many of these friends he began life, and passed hand in hand with them over youth's domain. Separated since from most of them, he has never forgotten those pleasant beginnings, and the glorious promise that then beckoned them on. Even in his darkness, those faces and those incidents return that made life then pleasant, tingeing his gloomy cell like the sunbeam that cheered the prison of Cervantes. He wishes them to buy his work, and thus show that the feeling he entertains is reciprocated. He needs their sympathy, but does not ask it as a beggar's alms; trusting to receive it as a tribute of love and a token of remembrance, that shall bless the giver as well as aid the receiver.

The author desires to express his gratitude to those kind

friends, who, on the previous and present occasions, have done so much to promote his interest and alleviate his sorrows; who have constantly studied his benefit, aiding him with their own means, and, through their representations, inciting others — many entire strangers — to help him. From his "heart of heart" he invokes for them the blessing promised those who seek to aid the unfortunate, whose feelings are attuned to the call of pity; praying that the good they do and have done him may return to them a thousand-fold. Though there is, of course, a precedence in claims upon his gratitude, he dare not be more specific, lest he do injustice to many friends whose offices have been later bestowed, but were none the less beneficent and welcome. Therefore he thanks them all in the sincerest manner, resting in the assurance of their continued regard.

DANIEL A. DROWN.

CONTENTS.

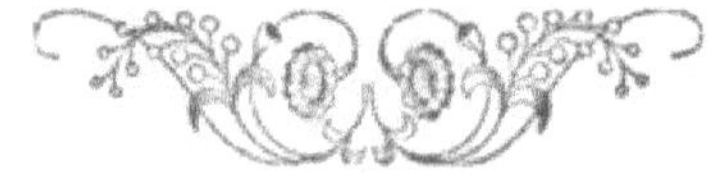

IDYLS OF STRAWBERRY-BANK.

IDYLS OF STRAWBERRY BANK.

THE RETURN OF THE SONS.

WHAT sounds are those that by my ear
  Come rushing up the glen?
Sweet music, rising high and clear,
  And tramp of marching men:
The festive gun and bell outpour
  A wealth of joyous tone,
That girts the woods of Sagamore
  With echoes like a zone.

What is it, neighbor? You can see, —
  Your eyes dread not the light:
Come show the mystery to me,
  Reflected in your sight.
Speak quickly, pray! O laggard! tell
  Why all this loud acclaim
Of joyous bell, with garrulous knell, —
  Of gun with throat of flame?

"It is our country's natal day;
  But more than common joy
Greeteth the morning's golden ray,
  Inspiring man and boy:
For from afar the 'SONS' return, —
  In serried ranks they move;
And in all hearts the glad fires burn
  Of welcome and of love.

"From every steeple 'welcome' rings;
  The morning sky is dim
With smoke suspent on airy wings,
  Like an unuttered hymn;
The nation's flag in blessing floats
  From every staff and tower;
And cheering from a thousand throats
  Makes jubilant the hour.

"I see the 'Sons' from Puddle Dock,
  And those from Christian Shore;
There Brimstone Hill's proud offspring flock;
  Rock Pasture comes once more;
From Point of Graves to Portsmouth Plains
  Their 'Sons' in gladness shout,
And not one nook of all remains
  A delegate without."

Neighbor, my heart is ill at ease;
  Oh! would the heavenly powers
Permit me to return like these,
  And revel in these hours!

But exile I, of saddest mould,
  Can never more return
Where life and joyousness unfold,
  And social altars burn.

God bless the "Sons"! — my brothers — all:
  Though I may never clasp
The hands of those I once could call,
  And feel their friendly grasp,
My heart here re-affirms the tie
  That early boyhood formed;
Though dull the pulse and dimmed the eye,
  'Tis with affection warmed.

But I will not in gloom despond:
  A gathering awaits
In the not very far beyond,
  Within the pearly gates.
There shall we all united throng,
  Where higher bliss shall sway,
And light and peace and joy and song
  Crown everlasting day.

"PAX VOBISCUM."

As sweet music in a valley
  Floats through shady aisles along,
Where the tinkling riplets' murmur
  Only joins the wavy song;
So, amid my own deep silence,
  Floated near, one stilly night,
Silvery strains, whose pleasant echoes
  Filled my heart with cheering light.

Clear the voice, and pure the accents,
  Which surprised my patient ear,
Ever listening, 'mid the stillness,
  Some good angel's wings to hear;
And they stirred within my bosom
  Thoughts of loved ones far away,
Who might send, with heavenly blessing,
  Shining words to light my day.

When the heart is pained and weary,
  Sad in its own solitude,
Is it not to memories sweetest
  By some soothing accents wooed?

Then the faintest loving echo
  Which the soul has ever heard
Vibrates, with a lengthened cadence,
  In each kindly-spoken word.

In the silent midnight hours,
  When I watch, all still and lone,
I would claim this grand benison —
PEACE BE WITH YOU ! — for my own ;
As if 'twere by angels spoken,
  I would feel its sacred power, —
Welcome, as to withering grasses
  Comes the cool, refreshing shower.

When life's storm shall gather fierceness,
  And its clouds shall grow more dark ;
When the foam-capped billows threaten
  To ingulf my trembling bark, —
Then, amid the angry waters,
  When my strength is wholly vain,
May strong faith "beyond the river"
  See the smiles of "Love" again !

May that blessed peace sustain me
  In the darkest, saddest hour
Which a Father's love bestoweth
  When the clouds of sorrow lower !
Let my heart, still loving, trusting,
  Safe repose in his own will ;
Knowing, in each fiery trial,
  That his love regards me still.

DEW ON THE GRASS.

How beautiful at morning light,
When summer winds are sighing,
To view the sparkling dewdrops bright
Upon the green turf lying,
With myriad rainbows circling round
These crystal forms, reposing
So humbly near the thirsty ground,
As night's moist wings are closing.

So pure and fresh the gorgeous scene,
They seem a diamond sea,
With isles of amethyst between,
And emerald shores to lea ;
O'er whose bright waters blue-birds skim,
As o'er a crystal cup,
To sweetly pour their morning hymn,
And pick the jewels up.

As silently as dews distil,
For nature kindly given,
So may thy grace my bosom fill
With choicest gifts from heaven ;

E'en though I lie recumbent, far
  Down in a suffering vale,
Let my dark night know one bright star,
  Nor let my courage fail.

Within this valley let me feel
  The dews which round me fall,
Which o'er my life so silent steal
  In blessings large and small ;
Let me behold in sorrow's night
  The jewels which descend,
Which yet shall sparkle in the light
  When life's short day shall end.

NOT LOST, NOR DEAD.

"To live in hearts we leave behind,
Is not to die." — *Campbell.*

SWEET thought! that in some loving hearts
Our names may be enshrined,
When cypress o'er our lowly forms
In sorrow may be twined,
Which silent speaks of absent ones,
Whose voices, hushed and still,
No more respond in gentle tones,
Which used the heart to thrill.

Safe in the chambers of the soul
Most cherished thoughts will dwell,
Abiding as the worth of those
We loved so long and well;
While Hope lights up the mourner's path
With its enlivening ray,
Which, like a morning-star, precedes
The glorious beams of day.

Not lost, nor dead; for mem'ry writes,
Upon a tablet pure,

Those virtues which shall never fade, —
  Whose fragrance shall endure ;
While Love, with her kind mantle, hides
  The errors of the past,
And gilds with light each generous deed,
  Whose lustre e'er shall last.

The sorrowing tears which grief distils
  For loved ones none can see,
Are sacred gems Affection brings
  From her rich treasury.
Like summer dews on starlit nights,
  Which feed the drooping flower,
They gently soothe the troubled heart
  With their subduing power.

But whether tears in silence fall,
  — Affection's fitting boon, —
Or smiles be seen because the goal
  Of bliss is reached so soon,
'Tis not to die, while yet we live
  In hearts sincere and true,
Who, longing, view the pearly gate
  To heaven we entered through.

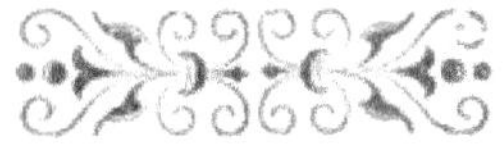

FRAGRANT FLOWERS.

Lovely flowers, ever beauteous,
  I would prize thy forms so fair,
Breathing out delicious odors
  Freely to the morning air,
With a thousand rainbows bending
  Round thy blushing petals bright,
Sparkling like the liquid diamonds
  In the rosy morning's light.

So may I, e'er looking upward
  To the starlit throne above,
Yield an offering, like sweet incense,
  Of true praises warmed with love.
May most gracious blessings ever
  On my heart like dews distil!
Then, more grateful, pure, and holy,
  Be my choice my Father's will.

Fragile flowers, with fringèd eyelids,
  Catch the sunbeams from the skies,
As bright favors which the morning
  Joys to send when evening dies;

Shooting out its golden arrows,
  As mid sunny clouds they play,
Scattering with its rosy fingers
  Fragrant treasures in their way.

So may I, most willing, ever
  Seize the truth, like sunbeams bright,
Shining through the darkened curtain,
  Which hideth heaven from my sight.
May I drink delicious nectar
  Dripping from an angel's wing,
With a heart prepared to welcome
  All the good his hands would bring!

Flowers may stay, and beauty linger,
  But a little season here,
Where are seen the clouds of sorrow
  And the sad, desponding tear;
But beyond this world of trouble,
  Destined never for the tomb,
Pleasures yielding blissful incense
  Shall for us forever bloom.

MY SUMMER MORNING SERENADE.

(3 O'CLOCK, A.M.)

WAKEFUL through the midnight hours,
  And at early dawn,
Wait I for the swelling chorus,
  Floating o'er the lawn.
Stately elms adorn my dwelling,
  Woodlands flourish near:
Whence proceeds the charming music
  Which delights my ear?

Ne'er before did I so welcome
  Such a choral throng:
Fragrant forests now seem flooded
  With their liquid song.
Bobolinks and robins carol
  Such delicious notes,
That a chime of sweetest music
  O'er the meadows floats.

When the shining car of morning
  Rises from the sea,
Then a thousand extra voices
  Swell the jubilee;

And their rapturous hearts seem breaking
With ecstatic bliss :
Who would not rejoice to welcome
Serenade like *this ?*

God be praised for birds and flowers,
Innocent and pure !
Melody and fragrance blending
Must for aye endure ;
Stirring up within our bosoms
Wells of gratitude,
Whose sweet waters murmur, praising
God, the ever good.

AN ECHO.

A SWEET little word in my heart I must cherish,
Euphonious and pleasant its tone;
And though many names from my memory may perish,
Not so can it be with thine own,
Not so can it be with thine own.

It tells me of friendship and constant devotion,
Which I love in my heart to enthrone,
So that, in its purest and deepest emotion,
Each wish may respond to thine own,
Each wish may respond to thine own.

It tells me of kindness and generous endeavor,
All fragrant as hay newly mown;
Of sympathy truest and purest, which ever
Possesses a charm all thine own,
Possesses a charm all thine own.

A silvery music thy name breathes, — as tender
As a flute in the eve softly blown;
So melodiously sweet that no artist can render
An echo so truly thine own,
An echo so truly thine own.

Affection and friendship and goodness seem blending
    To utter thy soul's purest tone,
So clear and so liquid, an angel seems lending
    His harp as a mate to thine own,
    His harp as a mate to thine own.

No name so deliciously pleasant can ever
    By me through life's journey be known,
Oh! then let no coldness or dark shadows sever
    Sunny memories linked with thine own,
    Sunny memories linked with thine own.

IN MEMORIAM.

HARRY HUBBARD KENNARD, DIED MAY 9, 1870, AGED 13 YEARS.

How oft across life's sunny skies
Some cloud of sorrow quickly flies,
Which casts a shadow o'er the heart;
While dews of grief their chill impart!
How oft within a home some flower
Unfolds rare beauties hour by hour;
When, like the passing of a breath,
Its petals fall in silent death!

And late, when brightest promise shone
About a dear and tender one,
And loving hearts and loving arms
Held him secure from earthly harms,
The gathering cloud unheeded grew,
Till hope's bright sun was hid from view;
And, from home's shelter where he lay,
The angels beckoned him away.

He pined with pain; but not a word
Of murmur e'er his young lips stirred:

Though fever might his bright eyes dim,
Its fierceness could not conquer him.
And so he smiled in hopeful cheer,
His courage grand, his love more dear ;
And, through the blessing that he shed,
A glory crowned his dying-bed.

At morning, when sweet violets smiled,
Passed on from earth the patient child ;
And in the realm of joy and peace
His gentle spirit found release, —
Release from pain, release from care,
In God's eternal love to share ;
Whose ways no human tongue can tell,
But who e'er doeth all things well.

But not in terror nor in gloom
Came he, the king of sable plume ;
No bitter grief, no cold despair,
Fell on the hearts that gathered there.
God's glory rested on the place,
And filled each soul with trust and grace,
That saw, through faith, the blessing strewn
Along the path the child had flown.

Sweet sympathy, in floral guise,*
Gave death the glow of paradise,

* The sympathy of loving friends, at the obsequies of dear Harry, found expression in floral tributes of the most exquisite character, that made the house of grief a bower of bloom.

And round his couch of dreamless rest
Shed perfumes from the gardens blest.
The wealth of loving hearts exhaled
In the pure fragrance that prevailed,
And, like a prayer of blessing said,
Followed the spirit that had fled.

He loved them so, those spotless flowers!
'Twas meet they fell in odorous showers
Upon that early tranquil bier, —
A sweet companionship and dear!
The blended blossoms to decay
Passed from fond, tearful eyes away;
But, brighter far than e'er before,
Their forms fond memory shall restore.

How cheering is this wealth of bloom!
Lifting the shadows from the tomb,
And seeming, to our loving eye,
A gleam of beauty from on high,
Where endless youth, eternal joy,
And bliss shall reign without alloy;
Where all that's fair and good and pure
Will in the smile of God endure.

"WE ALL DO FADE AS A LEAF."

ALL faded and gone are the whispering leaves,
Which wooed the warm sunshine at morn
With emerald lips wet with silvery dew,
Which in the cool evening were born.
All sparkling and bright
In rosy sunlight,
The vision was sweet to behold,
As trembling they spoke,
When the breezes awoke,
To clouds fringed with purple and gold.

The beautiful flowers, which at twilight's still hour
At vespers breathed fragrance for prayer,
Now silently sleep in their moss-covered graves,
Reposing in quietude there.
But sweet thoughts remain,
Which we love to retain ;
Remembering each kind, loving one
Who brought us sweet sprays
In warm summer days,
To bid all our sadness be-gone.

Like the leaflets of autumn, so manhood decays,
'Mid usefulness, beauty, and might;
And long-cherished scenes, fraught with innocent joys,
Must all fade away from our sight.
Rejoicing in health,
We seek after wealth,
All eager for pleasures below;
Yet leaves as they fall
Preach sermons to all,
And bid us true wisdom to know.

In heaven, the home of the ransomed, no more
Shall the changes of earth e'er be known;
But glory shall crown every beautiful scene,
Which we shall enjoy as our own.
Gay flowers will bloom,
Of richest perfume,
Nor fade in their beauty and prime,
And man nevermore,
On that blissful shore,
Shall know of the sorrows of time.

MUSINGS IN MAY.

When will the bounteous gifts of spring
  Revive my heart in lonely hours?
When will my quickened pulses thrill
  At songs of birds and breath of flowers?
When shall I roam the perfumed woods,
  And muse beside the crystal streams,
Or feast my soul where beauty smiles
  From vine-wreathed nooks and sunny gleams?

When will expanding buds and leaves
  Unfold their varied sweets to me,
Who, exiled long from Nature's charms,
  Long more and more those charms to see?
When will wild roses by the wall,
  And other children of the wood,
Allow my eyes once more to see
  What makes them smile in solitude?

Yet some will help me to enjoy
  The beautiful that blooms around, —
Will tell me of green, mossy dells,
  And where sweet violets are found.

These kindly acts will softly tell
  The promptings of a thoughtful love,
As one pure ray of welcome light
  Proves that bright sunshine glows above.

An opening bud or fragrant leaf
  Can bring the sweetest thoughts to me,
If it but whisper, low and clear,
  "I think of thee, — I think of thee."
May gentle spirits near me wait,
  To gladly cheer affliction's night,
And childlike trust forever gild
  All sorrow with a golden light!

My all I would repose in Him
  Who knows my feeble, struggling bark,
Sure that his love will safely guide,
  Though "home" be far, and night be dark.
Most gratefully may I receive
  Each proof of love "Our Father" sends,
And know, e'en in life's darkest hours,
  Sunshine with shadow ever blends!

WALKER'S MILL AND BRIDGE.

Then Mr. Peter Livius, by granting of the town,
Dammed up the creek called Islington, and laid the mill-bridge down,
Connecting worldly Strawberry-Bank with peaceful Christian-Shore,
And built the mill that we recall in dusty days of yore;
Also, the broad tide gate, that swung to check the waters' flow,—
A marvel of philosophy a hundred years ago.

Press Centenary Poem.

THE WILLOWS.

"The pendent willows by the sloping banks." — *Skillaber.*

Beneath those leafy willows green,
  In childhood's happy days,
I oft have found a welcome shade
  From too oppressive rays ;
And, when around my heated brow
  Refreshing breezes played,
Bright scenes have charmed my early dreams,
  In loveliest tints arrayed.

Their pliant branches have been made
  Obedient to my care ;
And they have kindly twined for me
  A sylvan grotto fair,
Where in my fairy grove I ate
  The strawberries I had found
But just behind my cool retreat,
  Upon the grassy mound.

* Sherburne's Wharf, Portsmouth, N.H.

There in youth's fond companionship
  The sportive moments flew ;
While in the tide that laved the shore,
  We bathed, — a happy crew, —
Or floated out there merrily
  Upon the gentle wave,
Having no thought of after-care,
  No boon of Fate to crave.

Before life's troubled cares can come,
  Or tears of sorrow fall,
How sweet the sparkling cup of joy,
  Which we would oft recall !
Each pleasant spot seems then to glow
  With pleasures ever new ;
And cherished memories then are born,
  Unlike the morning dew.

I loved those happy moments when
  My heart was light and free ;
When skies above and earth around
  Smiled lovingly on me ;
When in the future, distant far,
  I saw no clouds arise,
But golden sunshine light on all,
  With blessings from the skies.

Since then I've seen the shining goal
  Of which I early dreamed,
And found those pleasant scenes to be
  Not quite what once they seemed ;

But light and shade commingling where
  The prospect seemed most fair, —
Where tears and smiles together blend,
  And joy and pain and care.

Our lives are not quite all a dream,
  Though pleasures bud and bloom,
Like fragrant flowers, which often find
  A kind but early tomb ;
But far beyond these earthly scenes,
  Where fondest hopes decay,
A night of sadness shall be changed
  To an eternal day.

ANGEL VOICES.

WHEN night with her sombre shadows
  Broods in silence o'er the earth,
Where are scenes of bitter sadness,
  And of joyless, heartless mirth,
List I to sweet angel voices
  Stealing through the stilly air,
Welcome news most gladly bringing
  From their starlit dwelling fair.

When the heart is bowed in weakness
  By the weight of pain and grief,
Then I hear their pure lips telling
  Joyous things for my relief.
Love ordains the grievous chastening,
  Drawing children nearer home,
Where the soul, earth's fetters broken,
  Would most gladly haste to come.

Choicest flowers, crushed beneath us,
  Yield their hidden treasures rare,
Freely their sweet breath bestowing
  On the quiet morning air ;

So afflictions, when they press us,
  Like a burden, down to earth,
Only bid the heart's choice incense
  Brighter burn, and prove its worth.

Angel voices are above us
  And around us day by day,
Blessed words forever telling
  While from earth we look away.
To the weeping and the sorrowing
  Speak they of celestial things,
With the balm of consolation
  Sweetly dropping from their wings.

Stay, kind heavenly strangers, linger!
  As my willing guests abide :
Pearls of truth I then shall gather,
  If ye tarry by my side.
Cast your camps secure about me,
  As once round Jerusalem :
Choicest honors then shall crown me,
  Like a brilliant diadem.

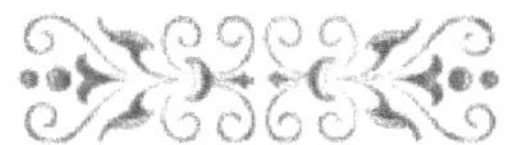

MUSINGS ON THE CLOSE OF THE YEAR.

How swiftly ebb the waves of time
  Along life's broken shore,
Revealing scenes of joy and pain,
  Which charmed and grieved before!
For memory wakes at twilight hour,
  While musing on the past,
Recalling bright and sunny days
  By shadows overcast.

Upon the tide of hope we sail
  Adown the flowing stream,
Inspired by warm and earnest zeal
  And many a thoughtful dream.
We see the goal towards which we haste
  Beaming with brilliant light,
Nor fear the unknown depths which hide
  The dangers of the night.

Life's voyage bids us fearless roam
  O'er many a stormy sea,
With boisterous winds still urging on,
  And breakers on the lea;

But, trusting to our chart and guide,
  We press unwearied on,
Nor rest till in the haven sure,
  The welcome prize is won.

But ere we reach that "open sea,"
  Beyond this earthly veil,
How many a toilsome course we make
  Where chilling storms assail!
But cherished hopes are often hid
  Beneath a threatening sky,
And many a weary day must pass
  Ere light will beam on high.

Blest be the hope which cheers our heart
  'Mid darkness, fears, and pain, —
There yet remains a welcome rest,
  An everlasting gain!
Beyond the ever-changing scene
  Of life's tempestuous tide,
A home is found, where purest joys
  Eternally abide.

THE ROSE WITHOUT A THORN.

In future days shall I recall
 One dewy summer morn,
When gentle hands then culled for me
 The rose without a thorn.
A token of sweet peace it came,
 In this my sorrow's night,
Where lovely flowers bloom unseen,
 E'en while they give delight.

" A rose without a thorn," she said,
 Then kindly gave it me,
When soon I found upon its leaves
 Were dews of sympathy, —
Sweet sympathy ! whose fragrant breath
 Proclaimed its heavenly birth,
Whose influence cheers the weary soul
 As dews the flowers of earth.

A kindly word, a gentle tone,
 With sympathy sincere,
A trifling deed, performed in love,
 Brings a good angel near ;

And, though her wings may not be seen,
  As spotless as the light,
They bring pure treasures for the soul,
  Which sparkle through the night.

Around life's chalice Friendship twines
  A wreath of evergreen,
Among whose tendrils delicate
  Fair little buds are seen,
Which, day by day, most lovingly
  Reveal their blushing forms,
Whose precious incense charms alike
  In sunshine and in storms.

Give me to drink from those sweet springs
  Which gush up from the heart
Of those who feel for others' woes,
  Who would all good impart;
Who lovingly would soothe my pain,
  Deploring every ill;
Who would with choicest, purest gifts
  My humblest chalice fill.

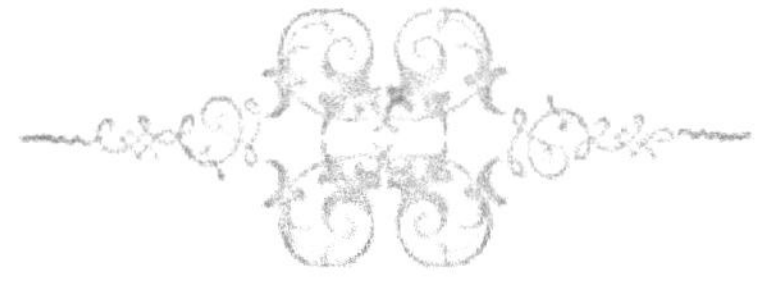

MAY MORNING.

MUSIC on the mountain, music in the dell,
Where the rippling streamlets, in soft cadence, tell
Of time's rolling current, in their gentle way,
Sparkling in the sunshine through the livelong day.

Music in the meadow, music on the lawn,
Where the blue-eyed blossoms wake to hail the dawn;
Peeping through the curtain of purest dewy light,
Which fair diamond fingers spread o'er them at night.

Music in the woodland, where the trembling trees
Whisper words of gladness to the passing breeze,
Laden with the praises of many a rosy lip,
Whose delicious nectar fairy forms might sip.

Now the queen of beauty wanders o'er the plain,
And the mossy hillocks smile with joy again,
As, with magic pencil, she paints glories where
Perfumes rise to heaven, like sweet words of prayer.

In the sloping valleys children of the wood
Greet her welcome footsteps in their solitude;

And, with grace so winning, coax a long delay,
Till the days of summer shall have passed away.

When the beams of morning chase the shades of night,
And a thousand anthems hail the glorious light,
May our hearts responsive catch the grateful tone,
Swelling high the chorus to our Father's throne!

Who with bounteous goodness shows his love and
power,
Making known his wonders freely every hour,
Teaching us in wisdom, from each blooming spring,
That immortal future time to all will bring.

FRIENDSHIP.

How sweet is Friendship! — like the balm
  Distilled from choicest flowers,
An influence like a heavenly charm
  To bless the fleeting hours, —
Yes, hours passed in solitude,
  Where darkness reigns around,
Where there is known but little good,
  And many ills are found.

Still let me often hear thy voice,
  Which gently whispers peace;
And let my troubled heart rejoice,
  And strains of sadness cease.
Still speak to me of pleasant things, —
  Of faith and hope and joy:
Then shall I rise on lightsome wings
  Where pains no more annoy.

Thy soothing tones with peace beguile
  The weary hours of pain,
And make the lonely sufferer smile,
  And joy to come again.

Like voices of the stilly night,
  Glad spirits come and go ;
And tell of things in visions bright,
  Which dreams reveal below.

Let me feel friendship's magic power,
  Whate'er my prospects be,
Kindly as dewdrops kiss the flower,
  Or moonbeams gild the sea :
Then shall I feel thy presence near,
  Though clouds obscure my skies,
And no more dreary, dark hours fear,
  Till heaven shall greet mine eyes.

A GRATEFUL RESPONSE TO THE PORTSMOUTH CORNET BAND.

THRICE welcome were the harmonies which broke
Upon my ear at twilight hour,
When from the realms of dreamland quick I woke,
Enchanted by their magic power:
Those cheerful notes like silver bells I heard
Ring merry chimes within this gloom:
My weary heart with joy once more was stirred;
And sunshine filled my darkened room.

Sweet memories of departed days once more
Recalled the songs that then were sung
With youthful friends of buoyant heart, before
My harp upon the willows hung;
And yet again I live in manhood's prime,
Forgetting all my loss and pain,
While your delicious notes, like summer-time,
Bloom into life with each refrain:

For once again your generous sympathy
Has poured inspiring strains for me;
As 'twere a benediction from the sky
You gave the friend you could not see.

I claimed it ; and, though many a deed may fail
  To grace the page of memory,
This pleasant thought I know will sure prevail,
  Which reads, "Ye did it unto me."

How blest thy mission, thus to sweetly cheer
  With tuneful notes the burdened heart,
When life's fair scenes would else seem lone and drear
  Bereft of thy soul-stirring art!
How many a joy thy welcome advent wakes
  In weary hours of solitude,
In which delight e'en now my heart partakes,
  With sincere gratitude imbued.

CONTENTMENT, OR THE BLEST JEWEL.

I ASKED a young man blest with health,
Whose star of life was bright,
To whom all future prospects seemed
To dance in golden light,
If he this jewel kept concealed
Within his hopeful breast, —
If at this stage he soon should pause,
His soul would find sweet rest.

"Ah, no!" he said: "the goal beyond
Invites my hastening feet.
Distinguished honors wait me there:
Life's warfare I must meet.
I long to see the golden light
Encircling my fair name,
And read on tablets deep engraved
The blazon of my fame."

I asked a rich man, blest with wealth,
And all things good and fair,
To whom the skies looked bright above,
— No shadows lingering there, —

If, blest with wealth, he there would wait
  While Time's swift car rolled on,
And be contented with his lot
  Till life's brief sands were run.

" Ah, no ! " he said : " though pleasures lie
  Within my grasp each day,
The wheel of fortune quick may turn,
  And sweep my all away.
A ' little more ' I must obtain
  Against an evil hour ;
And then secure will I repose,
  Nor fear the tyrant's power."

I asked a poor man, struggling hard
  To breast the storms of life,
Whose surging billows almost hide
  Him 'neath their angry strife,
If he had found that goodly tree
  Whose precious fruit so fair,
If tasted, would all joy afford,
  And peaceful offerings bear.

" Ah, no ! " he said : " the rich have wealth,
  — With ease it can provide, —
While I toil on with grief opprest
  From morn till eventide.
And when the shadows gather fast,
  My wasting strength quite spent,
I lay me down 'mid tears and pain, —
  No : I am not content."

I asked the Christian, who is found
  Among the poor and great, —
Oft clothed in garments coarse and worn,
  Sometimes in robes of state, —
If he had found the jewel bright,
  More prized than rubies rare,
Which would, as a pure treasure kept,
  Yield comfort everywhere.

"Oh, yes!" he said, while radiant smiles
  Illumed his happy face:
"That priceless gem has long been mine, —
  The gift of sovereign grace;
Because, at peace within, my heart
  Invites no anxious care:
But sweet Content her offering brings,
  And makes her dwelling there."

PEACE, BE STILL.

When o'er life's sky a curtain deep
  Close hides the genial light
Which ever shines dark clouds above
  With rays most pure and bright;
When sorrows crowd around our way,
  And tears our chalice fill,
Then gladly hears the burdened soul
  The accents, "Peace, be still."

When love's sweet bonds are severed wide,
  And cherished friends depart,
Who, though so pure and spotless here,
  Might not escape death's dart;
When poignant grief or dull despair
  Their bitter dews distil,
Then softly as sweet music comes
  The gentle "Peace, be still."

Like balm from Gilead freely sent,
  Or fruits from Eschol's vine,
They bid our drooping spirits rise,
  And cause the face to shine;

While living streams forever flow,
  Free as the mountain rill :
Then in most soothing tones we hear
  The accents, " Peace, be still."

May He who rules the raging storm,
  Who bids the billows sleep,
Uphold us with his outstretched hand,
  And ever near us keep.
How would our hearts within us burn,
  And joy our bosoms fill,
Could we above life's tempests hear
  His holy " Peace, be still " !

BEAUTIFUL IS MOONLIGHT.

BEAUTIFUL is moonlight, flashing through the trees,
Kissing trembling leaflets ruffled by the breeze,
Gilding branch and flower with a mellow hue,
Giving each new beauty, charming to the view.
With a chain of silver earth and heaven unite ;
Peaceful thoughts fly homeward, up the shining height :
Thence our hearts will follow to that other shore,
Where true beauty lingers, fadeless evermore.

Beautiful is moonlight resting on the billow,
Softly as an infant on its downy pillow ;
The blue waters bridging with a golden way,
As if paved with jewels by the god of day.
O'er this shining pathway fancy oft will roam,
And behold pure spirits passing to their home,
By the fragrant zephyrs swiftly fanned along,
While the blessed angels chant their sweetest song.

O'er the fields of clover swift the moonbeams glide,
Shooting o'er dark valleys where the streamlets hide,
Lighting up the meadows, where the crystal dew
Sparkles on the herbage, cooling it anew.

Through the woods and orchards their glowing track
is seen,
Smilingly " bo-peeping " through the branches green ;
While the fragrant blossoms, touched with silver glow,
Whisper to each other approvingly, I know.

What a flood of glory bathes the fields and flowers !
What inspiring stillness charms the midnight hours !
What a gush of feeling wells up from the soul,
While the grateful anthems through its arches roll !
And the very silence beautifies the scene,
Blending all the glory with a joy serene,
As the gentle whispers of a Father's love
Lead the willing spirit to its home above.

Beauteous moonlight evenings have a silent power,
Soothing oft the weary in a troubled hour,
When inspired voices sing within the breast,
Telling their glad story, — perfect, endless rest.
Let my fancy revel with the moonbeams bright,
Though I do not gaze upon their silver light,
By and by made perfect, on the " shining shore,"
I'll view all its glories, happy evermore.

"LET THERE BE LIGHT."

THICK darkness brooded o'er the slumbering earth;
While silent at the gate of Morning slept
The warder, with his golden quiver full
Of shining arrows barbed with crimson light,
Which lay concealed as in a sacred shrine,
Awaiting royal hands to bring them forth.
Above his brow, a crown of purest white,
Inlaid with brilliants and rose-tinted pearls,
In silent grandeur rested, like a cloud
Of diamonds girt with bands of rainbow hue,
Whose beauty, veiled in deepest shade, refused
To cast a glory o'er the dismal scene.
Above, no star-gemmed canopy o'erspread
The wide expanse, on which are seen the steps
Of angels, as in countless hosts they march
On azure pavements round the sapphire throne;
Below, no signs of life or beauty stirred
The praise of seraphs, who, with folded wings,
In wonder e'er behold the wondrous power
Of Him who maketh all things good and fair.
On either hand dark curtains hung, where lay,
Entombed within the wide, unmeasured space,

A priceless, unknown jewel, destined yet
Upon the signet-ring of Him to shine
Whose royal seal proclaims the wisdo m, love
And matchless skill of the great Architect.
Upon the face of mighty waters dwelt
A cloud, which, in its hollow chambers drear,
Concealed the restless billows capped with foam,
And hushed its echoes in deep solitude.
The searching eye of Deity, with whom
Alike the darkness and the light are one,
Beheld the lonely scene, so desolate ;
While on his ear low moans from heaven above
And earth beneath fell piteously distinct,
Like the sad wailings of the wintry wind,
As, in their prison-house enchained, they sighed
In mutual grief for life and light unknown :
Then, moved by love and power infinite,
In majesty he gave the great command,
— And yet commanded from his throne no one, —
"*Let there be light!*" and instantly "light was."

THE BASKET OF STRAWBERRIES.

Berries sweet and berries red
  Generous hands have brought to-day,
Gathered where the robins fed,
  Near the fields of new-mown hay;
Luscious in their tempting prime,
  Their rich fragrance lingers near
While I tell in hasty rhyme
  What now makes the gift more dear.

Some kind friend who views the sun,
  Birds and trees and brooks and flowers,
Gorgeous shades when day is run,
  Rosy tints at morning hours,
Thought of my e'er darkened room,
  Where bright sunshine smileth not,
Glad to prove, though veiled in gloom,
  I by no means was forgot.

Even now methinks I see
  Snow-white hands divide the leaves,
Where the strawberries daintily
  Hide beneath their sheltering eaves.

But for a sweet, gentle tone,
Like low breathings of a flute,
I should think snow-birds had flown
'Mong the vines in search of fruit.

Blessings ever be on those,
Who, though wealth and ease obtain,
Ne'er forget a sufferer's woes,
Drawing from their hearts' deep main ;
Whose pure waters bright and cool
As sweet balm refresh and cheer,
When the burdened billows roll,
Crested with both pain and fear.

Benisons on each kind heart
Who would lift a veil of woe,
And by cheerful tones impart
Happy thoughts the sad to know.
Life to such is not a dream,
When each deed fresh pleasure brings :
To our grateful souls they seem
Angels, but with folded wings.

SLEEP.

WHEN Night with unseen fingers draws
  Her curtain o'er the sky,
Embroidered with those brilliant gems,
  Which shine so pure on high,
Within its darksome shade there comes
  The messenger of rest,
Who in deep silence folds his wings
  Above each weary breast.

With noiseless footsteps soft and light,
  Like flakes of falling snow,
He ventures near, and lays his wand
  Upon my aching brow.
Forgetful of those varied cares
  With which earth's labor teems,
I tread the flowery paths of peace,
  Found in the realm of dreams.

I oft recline in lovely bowers,
  And muse contented there,
Where charming fragrance, freely breathed,
  Pervades the balmy air.

I wander through fair meadows green,
Where modest violets grow,
And through the woodland's spicy shade,
Where dancing streamlets flow.

I list enchanted to those strains
Which sweetly charm the mind,
Struck from a harp by unseen hands,
And borne upon the wind:
I catch the burden of a song,
As floats the echo by,
Whose heavenly cadence breathes of joys
Which never, never die.

I meet again the loved and true,
Whose voice once cheered me here,
And list to hear those accents pure
Which once brought heaven near.
Content and blest, I thus would stay,
And know no harm nor fears,
Where angel spirits always dwell,
To chase desponding tears.

But Sleep extends her gentle wings,
Obedient to her laws,
And Night before the gates of morn
Her curtain dark withdraws.
I wake amid life's toils and cares,
And find not all a dream;
But, though dark clouds may round us lower,
Blest rays of hope still gleam.

IN THE VALLEY.

In the valley, where the shadows
  Linger in the woodland bowers,
Veiling in their dreamy silence
  Clustering vines and fragrant flowers,
    Would I love to roam ;
Listening to the murmuring streamlets
  O'er their pebbly pathways flowing,
As they dance to silvery music,
  On their winding mission going
    Toward their ocean home.

Lilies in the crystal waters,
  Dripping with their diamond tears ;
Daisies on the mossy hillocks,
  Smiling when the sun appears,
    Would I love to own ;
Seeking, too, the laughing cowslips
  Skirting all the meads around, —
Golden flowers with sunny faces,
  Vying with sweet violets found
    O'er the green banks strown.

Songsters in the branches chirping,
In the cool and balmy air,
Welcoming the tints of morning
In a concert sweet and rare,
Would delight me long ;
While content among the bowers,
Free from grief and pain and care,
Drinking fragrance from the flowers,
Would I chant pure praises there,
In one grateful song.

In another valley dreary
Must I suffering, patient wait,
Where no purple tints of morning
Ope to me the Orient gate
While I tarry here ;
But beyond these dark surroundings,
Where immortal flowers shall bloom, —
Where no tears nor pain nor sorrows
Shall be known beyond the tomb, —
Is my rest, so dear.

In sweet vales "beyond the river,"
Redolent with choicest balm
From the "tree of life" proceeding,
Which can my lone spirit calm,
Shall I shortly roam ;
And beside the cool, "still waters"
Pluck the fadeless, purest flowers,
As they smile, like Eden's treasures,
From enchanting heavenly bowers,
In my long-sought home.

MEMORY AND HOPE.

STILL dark shadows fall around me,
  As I pensive muse alone,
Where relentless chains have bound me,
  While life's summer days have flown.
Though in this low vale I tarry,
  Shut out from the fair blue sky,
Yet within my heart I carry
  Pictures that can never die.

Where the woodland's shady hollows
  Stretch out in long aisles away,
There imagination follows
  Till I almost see the day
Smile in beauty all around me;
  While the bowers of evergreen
With their fragrant breath surround me,
  Blessing all the pleasant scene.

Through the scented, tangled wild-wood,
  Memory wanders many a day,
Where in buoyant, happy childhood
  With my mates I used to stray;

And I hear again glad voices
  Wandering through the silent shade;
When my heart once more rejoices
  That not all which charmed must fade.

Though I cannot cull those flowers
  Which once cheered both heart and sight,
Nor with dear ones share those hours
  Which ne'er failed to give delight,
Now and then a blossom falleth
  From my fancy's slender tree,
Which some pleasant scene recalleth,
  Fair to those who think of me.

Then I seem to live again
  In those sunny days of yore,
Waking, with a sense of pain,
  Still upon the hither shore.
And I look "beyond the river"
  Where the heart's chief treasures lie,
Longing to "abide forever,"
  Clothed with immortality.

MAY-FLOWERS.

SWEET gifts of May, fair blossoms of the spring!
Your fragrant breath proclaims to me
That sunny days have smiled on thee,
And warmed thee into life again,
'Mid melting snows and April rain;
And now my muse thy praise would sing.

What pleasant thoughts your dewy petals bring
Of former days of sun and shower,
When blooming health blest every hour;
When bud and blossom, leaf and tree,
In early spring gave joy to me!
To all those years what sunny memories cling!

Fair buds of May, what trust thy frail lives teach!
Though veiled beneath the drifted snow,
A calm repose ye found below
Green ferns and mosses of the wood,
Content with thine own solitude,
Sure that the sun's bright beams thy couch would reach,

And smile as mothers smile upon the face
Of little ones in peaceful rest,
Glad to obey their first behest,
When new life wakens with the light,
When angels cease their watch by night,
And give to each fair child new strength and grace.

Sweet children, come! come, whisper in my ear
With fragrant breath the lesson taught
By Him whose loving care is fraught
With precious blessings, numbered o'er
For all his children, rich and poor,
That I may ever feel his presence near.

Oh! let my faith be strong in him each day;
So that in every darksome hour,
When shadows round my tent may lower,
Or when my sky glows bright with love,
Proceeding from the throne above,
I e'er may learn sweet trust from "flowers of May."

LIGHT IN DARKNESS.

TO MY FRIENDS.

SOME with music seek my pleasure,
Kindest thoughts joined to each measure.
Sympathy most true they bring me,
Sweeter than the notes they sing me.

Thoughtful deeds and words most tender
Are the tribute some would render
When my heart is sad and weary,
And life's journey seems most dreary.

Some bestow their choicest flowers,
Thus to cheer the lonesome hours;
Wishing, with the sweets revealing,
Angel forms might near be stealing,

With inspiring thoughts to bless me,
And with loving words caress me;
While in pain I'm ever pining
For the brightness clearly shining.

With pure hearts and faces smiling,
All foreboding fears beguiling,
Some, their sheaves of plenty bringing,
Set my grateful heart to singing.

So my generous friends, combining,
Bid me view the silver lining
Which dark shadows were concealing
Till the time for its revealing.

While our Father's love protecting,
Every good for us selecting,
But allows the clouds of sorrow
To precede heaven's bright to-morrow.

ONE LITTLE WORD.

WHAT'S in a word, a smile, a tear?
  What's in a gentle tone?
I answer, What is in a rose
  With all its fragrance gone?
What's in the grasping of the hand?
  What in a fond caress?
A language spoken without words,
  That proves its power no less.

One little word I like to hear,
  Of such a pleasant tone,
It comes so sweetly to my ear
  When suffering and alone.
It signifies a willing mind,
  A kindness pure and free,
As if 'twere "pleasure" to perform
  Aught undertook by thee.

It speaks a silent sympathy
  Beneath an uttered tone,
Which makes it easy oft to ask
  To have some favor done.

It seems to make one's burden less
  When cheerful words are near,
Which but attend on ready hands,
  That make each act more dear.

I gaze not on the golden beams
  Of brightness others see:
My sun shines out from words and deeds
  Most kindly shown to me.
A cheerful "yes," when racked with pain,
  Is music to my ear :
I gather from the silvery tone
  An angel form is near.

It proves amid external things
  Dwells living sympathy,
So welcome when one can but be
  Dependent, never free.
Through all my life may friendly words
  And pleasant sounds unite
To make up in sweet harmony
  What cannot bless my sight!

MY WELCOME SERENADE.

Though remote from town, musicians who may be in the vicinity of his home, favor him with serenades that greatly cheer him. The following was in response to a party of singers, "camping out" at Sagamore Creek, who paid him a visit at twilight, and sang him songs and hymns, at which he was particularly delighted. The poem breathes the grateful feeling of the author on the occasion. — Ed.

Still remembered, though dark shadows
  Yet obscure my weary way;
For the sunshine of your gladness
  Cheered my heart anew to-day:
And I welcomed the sweet offering
  Generous friends thus proffered me,
While unseen I eager listened
  To each measure gratefully!

Earnest seeking health and pleasure
  Where the cooling breezes blow,
Thoughtfully a while you lingered
  Proofs of kindliness to show
One who cannot pluck the flowers
  Which adorn your pleasant way,
Nor behold those scenes of beauty
  Which invite a long delay.

Let me hear the lively chorus
  When the cheerful throngs go by,
Song and laughter freely blending
  With the invalid's low sigh.
Life must not have too much sadness,
  Though the cloud of sorrow lowers;
Cheering beams of sunny brightness
  Smile between the April showers.

And my heart is yet responsive
  To the sounds of joy and mirth,
To the beauty and the gladness
  Which in innocence have birth:
But I gaze beyond the river,
  Where are joys unknown before;
Where shall come no night of weeping,
  E'er to dim that shining shore.

SAGAMORE, July 29, 1869.

AUTUMN LEAVES.

Autumn leaves now gently falling
  To the soil which gave them birth,
With their gorgeous colors blending
  Like a rainbow dropped to earth,
Speak in accents sad but truthful
  Of those hopes we hold most dear,
Whispering, like the sweetest music,
  Blessed thoughts the heart to cheer.

First, in vigor bright and healthful,
  With their emerald beauty dressed,
Fanned by zephyrs richly laden
  With the odors of the West,
Sunny skies above them bending,
  Sport they all in life's young morn ;
To each beauteous scene bestowing
  Eden's freshness, glory born.

Now with vestures richly varied,
  — Russet, orange, green, and red, —
Crowning all the woods with splendor
  Ere they seek their mossy bed ;

One by one they droop and wither,
  Touched by autumn's chilling frost,
Till bright leaves with silver linings
  Are in all their beauty lost.

So life's scenes are often changeful,
  Varying with the light and shade :
Where the fairest flowers blossom,
  There the thorn its home hath made.
But though clouds may dim our prospects,
  And our fondest hopes decay,
Brighter is the day before us
  When the night is chased away.

Like cool autumn's fading leaflets,
  We must heed our final call,
When the silver cord is loosened,
  And the shadows round us fall :
Then with pure, angelic beauty,
  Free from every earthly stain, —
Then the soul shall find its treasures
  When its springtime comes again.

BRING FLOWERS.

BRING flowers to me each sunny morn,
  Bespangled with the dew ;
For gifts like these, so pure and fair,
  Awaken thoughts of you.
I'll breathe their fragrance floating near
  When silent and alone,
And bless the hand that gathered them
  To make them all mine own.

Bring flowers, for they sweetly tell
  Of blooming meads around ;
Of pleasant nooks, where velvet leaves
  Of every shade are found.
Bring lilies from the crystal stream,
  Wild roses from the wall,
And many a pet from woodland homes,
  Which former days recall.

I love the mild and gentle breath
  Which wakes the buds of spring,
And bids the fragrant violets bloom,
  To which fond memories cling.

E'en now I think I see them smile
  Upon the hillocks green,
Just peeping with cerulean eyes
  The golden moss between.

I love the welcome summer, too,
  Replete with beauteous flowers,
Which scatter incense through the air,
  And charm the twilight hours.
Like sisters, hand in hand they glide
  To beauty's gay boudoir:
One turns the key with fragrant hand,
  The other opes the door.

Within a treasury of sweets
  Would I in quiet rest,
And hold some blushing roses close
  To my sad, troubled breast;
Then should I dream of lovely bowers,
  Where health and beauty stay,
While speed the joyous, happy hours
  Throughout the livelong day.

When I am gone, let sweet flowers smile
  Above my lowly form,
Because a weary soul has passed
  Beyond life's fitful storm.
With perfumed lips they plainly tell
  Of life beyond the tomb,
Where God shall with a holy light
  The darkest way illume.

JESUS, MY HOPE.

WITH hope in Christ, I fear no ill,
For his right hand supports me still;
Though trials here my paths surround,
I boast in him my strength is found.
He will supply sustaining grace
To those who seek with love his face.

When clouds around my tent prevail,
And gloomy thoughts my peace assail;
When cherished hopes are severed here,
Where strong hearts know the bitter tear,
In him a safe retreat I find:
A refuge from each stormy wind.

When bound by sad affliction's chain,
Oppressed with grief, beset with pain;
When tedious days new troubles weave,
So that to dust my soul would cleave,
One lively hope illumes the night:
Jesus is near, though veiled from sight.

When joy and love expand their wings,
My heart with wonder often sings,
That I have found, in one so dear,
A bosom friend, forever near,
Who will his promises defend,
And ne'er forsake, though time should end.

In Jesus all my peace is found:
He makes my purest joys abound;
He bids me at his table wait
To share the banquet free and great.
I tarry long: my soul is fed
By angel hands with heavenly bread.

His presence I more highly prize
Than all the gold beneath the skies:
My birthright here I would not lose
For all the honors I could choose:
More precious far than rubies rare,
His words my cherished treasures are.

Blest Jesus! I would see thy face,
In whom I trust for every grace:
Thy friendly counsels I would hear,
With cheerful heart and willing ear.
Oh! grant me still thy power divine:
Thine arms of love still round me twine.

FALLING SNOW.

In airy crowds from the regions above,
Silent and pure as a whisper of love,
These wingèd sprites, in their chariots white,
Descend to earth like an army of light.
They pitch their tents on the mountain's side,
In vales beneath, where the streamlets glide:
They rest content in the tops of the trees,
And fearlessly sport with the jubilant breeze.
Like knights in ermine with glistening spears,
They sally forth when the storm-king appears,
And scale high walls, standing never aloof,
But post their sentries on casement and roof.
Their countless hosts in battalions press on
So fast that triumph is sure to be won;
And pæans loud are then borne by the gale
O'er white-crowned turrets, through each lonely vale,
Through forests dark to the wild-rolling sea,
To plunge in the mists of immensity.
They reign supreme in the shadows of night,
And safely roam by the moon's silvery light,
With sandals light, over meadow and hill,
And dance with glee o'er the ice-fettered rill.

With downy crests, with the wind for their steed,
They ride unchecked where their fancies lead ;
Approaching slowly where bright fires gleam,
To pass away as a beautiful dream.
With fingers soft they oft play with our hair,
Departing soon ere we know they are there ;
And try in glee to awaken a smile,
While dancing close to our eyelids the while.
Untamed and free they oft dare to sip
Nectarian sweets from the pure ruby lip
Of maidens fair, who would blush to bestow
A gift so freely to others we know ;
But caught at last they do penance in tears,
And vanish soon as the birth of their fears.
With purest lips they kiss the blue stream,
Then melt away in a sweet, dewy dream,
And slumber on, wishing never to rise,
Till silent, unseen, they ascend to the skies.

THE PISCATAQUA.

Piscataqua! that mighty tide;
With all our youthful thoughts allied,
Yet rolls its eddying waves along,
Untiring, ceaseless, swift and strong,
As when, with pole, and hook, and string,
We fished for pollock by the "Spring."

B. P. S.

"Over the river's broad expanse,
    Here and there a boat is darting,
Swelling sails and foaming bows,
    Life unto the scene imparting.
Humble market-wherry there
    Lags along with lazy oar;
Here the lordly packet-boat
    Dashes by with rushing roar."

"Sail on the Piscataqua," by James Kennard, Jr.

THE BETTER LAND.

THERE is a land, a better land,
  Beyond this earthly scene,
Whose distant shores we long to see,
  Though dark waves roll between.
We wish to view those flowery banks,
  Washed by the living stream,
And gaze upon those wondrous things,
  Unknown to Fancy's dream.

We wish to breathe the balmy air,
  With fragrance e'er replete,
And see the crystal dewdrops fall
  Like diamonds at our feet ;
We long to gaze the landscape o'er,
  All spangled with pure gems,
And pluck the blushing roses there,
  Without their thorny stems.

We long to hear those heavenly strains
  The angels love to sing,
To which the golden harps attune
  Their sweetest offering.

Most gladly would we lend an ear
  To the eternal song,
And join to swell the chorus loud,
  With all the ransomed throng.

No sickness, pain, nor death shall there
  Our ceaseless pleasures mar;
For sin shall be forever kept
  With all its ills afar.
Unfading beauty then shall press
  Her signet on each brow,
And blooming health no more decay
  Like fragile flowers, as now.

We long to pluck the precious fruit
  From the blest tree of life,
Whose wondrous leaves forever heal
  The nations of their strife.
We then shall feast on angels' food,
  And have them for our guests;
For, in that glorious world of light,
  The curse no longer rests.

All tears shall then be wiped away:
  Their fountain shall be dry;
And ne'er in secret shall be known
  The burden of a sigh.
All doubts and gloomy thoughts shall flee
  Like leaves before the wind,
Nor leave the faintest shadow there
  To cloud a peaceful mind.

Unequalled glories there shall pass
  Before our constant view,
Which shall our senses never tire,
  Because forever new.
Each beauteous prospect shall conspire
  To give us fresh delight:
Ear hath not heard, eye hath not seen
  One-half the blissful sight.

We long to gaze on the new earth,
  — That promised "better land," —
And, with immortal honors blest,
  Amid its wonders stand.
Then let me end my journey here,
  And with rejoicing come
To claim my birthright in that world, —
  My glorious heavenly home.

THAT GENTLE VOICE.

As music comes at eventide,
  On fragrant zephyrs borne,
Most welcome to the lonely heart
  Oft by deep sorrow torn ;
So grateful comes that gentle voice,
  Which oft my sadness quells,
With mellow accents soft and sweet,
  Like chimes from silver bells.

That gentle voice has power to soothe
  When troublous thoughts arise
Like secret foes to mar our peace,
  And dim life's sunniest skies.
Like sunshine on the summer cloud,
  Their shadows briefly last, —
A few bright jewels only dropped
  As tribute to the past.

When weary hours in dreaded pain
  Make up the sufferer's lot ;
When earth's fair scenes can no more yield
  One bright forget-me-not, —

How sweet amid surrounding gloom
  To hear one gentle word,
Which kindest sympathy reveals,
  From hearts with pity stirred!

Let me but hear some kindly words
  From loving hearts and true,
Then all my days on earth are blest,
  Though chosen friends are few:
Let me but hear a gentle voice,
  Which no sad tidings brings,
Which speaks in accents soft and sweet,
  Of pure and holy things;

Let me but know that bright flowers bloom
  Around my pathway still,
Which breathe of purity and truth,
  And God's most righteous will;
Though shadows then may thickly lower
  Around my tent each day,
A glorious future, far more bright,
  Shall chase my night away.

A TRIFLING GIFT.

A TRIFLING gift, — one little rose
Just bursting into bloom ;
For such the little stranger was
That came, with sweet perfume,
To cheer me in my loneliness,
And drive sad thoughts away, —
A foretaste of those gardens fair,
Whose blossoms ne'er decay.

One little rose ! and yet how much
This welcome gift I prize !
No golden treasure ever seemed
So beauteous to my eyes.
The kindly tone and look it bore,
To other charms gave birth,
Enhancing, as they clustered there,
Its own intrinsic worth.

How oft one kind and gentle word
Will peace and joy impart,
And make the warmest sunshine glow
Upon the saddest heart !

How oft one trifling gift will speak,
  Where words are needed not!
The heart soon learns the thought to read
  That seeks to soothe its lot.

Sweet memories linger round each flower
  Which friendship ever gave,
A holy incense floating o'er
  Each little perfumed grave.
From every withered leaf and bud
  Flows forth a touching strain,
Till voice and lute in memory's ear
  Echo the soft refrain.

Still come to me in all your pride,
  Ye blushing roses bright!
Each petal can a page unfold
  My spirit to delight.
I joy to feel your presence near,
  Surrounding me with love,
Like holy angels, freely sent
  With blessings from above.

THE MARCH OF THE FROST KING.

Bright are the colors the Frost King is weaving
  Now in the mantle which robes all the trees:
Delicate touches his fingers are leaving,
  Silently kissed by the cool evening breeze, —
Purple and orange and pale-tinted yellow,
  Varied with meshes of bright scarlet shade,
Green-tinted borders relieving its fellow,
  Skilfully wrought in the garment now made.

From a light groundwork of russet is gleaming
  Flickering shadows of amber and gold,
Which, like a flame, in the sunlight is beaming,
  Oft as his robes in the breezes unfold.
Silver-leafed maples and ash-trees are glowing,
  Blushing so deeply as morning steals on,
Oaks all their various beauties are showing,
  Smiling as if all their glory was won.

Now through the woodlands the Frost King is going,
  Gathering strength for a final display;
Myriads of troops to his standard are flowing,
  Eager to join in the brilliant array.

Music, though pensive and mellow, is sounding,
  Floating o'er meadow, o'er valley and hill ;
Summer's fair soldiers their weapons are grounding,
  Ere they shall sleep by the ice-fettered rill.

Thus we move onward 'mid life's changeful battle,
  Shoulder to shoulder through earth's busy strife,
Hearing the echoes which round us e'er rattle,
  Always attending the cares of this life ;
But let us whisper kind words at our parting,
  Gladly to cheer every soul on his way ;
Strength for the conflict and counsel imparting
  While in the valley of sorrow we stay.

Changes must come ; for the leaves are now falling ,
  Shadows bespeak, too, the close of the day ;
But in the future sweet voices are calling,
  Angels of mercy will smile on our way.
Then, when our warfare is peacefully ended,
  — Trouble and sorrow and trials all o'er, —
Contentment and joy and triumph all blended,
  Will crown us, victorious in bliss, evermore.

ON RECEIVING A FRAMED BOUQUET OF AUTUMN LEAVES.

AUTUMN leaves, with tints all glowing,
  As they fell within the wood,
Kindly hands have brought, bestowing,
  To relieve my solitude.

Through fringed eyelids brightly glancing,
  As the rain-drops bathed each form,
Once these children frail were dancing
  To the music of the storm ;

Smiling as their glistening faces
  Oft were kissed by sunshine bright,
Conscious of their airy graces,
  Which they knew must give delight.

Once they whispered to each other
  In the moonlight near the stream,
As pet sisters to a brother,
  When they know life's first sweet dream.

Now they lie content, reposing
  In a quiet, long embrace,
While I read, when day is closing,
  Telltale blushes in each face.

Now perhaps they list sweet voices,
  Which they welcomed by the shore,
As a lover's heart rejoices
  To recount his wooings o'er.

Let them rest in peaceful slumbers,
  Let each know blest joys again,
While fond memory's tablet numbers
  Blessings o'er like drops of rain.

Let them smile when morning greets them,
  As if they were green once more,
Sigh when a mild zephyr meets them,
  Whispering some sweet secret o'er.

Dream, dream on! though ne'er waking,
  Though each smile reveals to-day
That I, too, these scenes forsaking,
  Like you, soon must pass away.

WINTER IS COMING.

COLD winter is coming! His heralds proclaim
Now through the tall forests the sound of his name:
They break the deep silence which soothed the wild-
flowers,
Which peeped forth in sunshine to drink the warm
showers,
And scatter the leaflets with wild, sweeping blast,
Regardless of beauty, or scenes of the past,
When through the green wildwood a silvery strain
Repeated its echoes again and again.

The fragrance of summer has gladdened each heart,
And visions of beauty have outrivalled art;
Ripe autumn has yielded its full golden sheaves,
And left a bright smile as it kissed the green leaves:
But each sunny hollow and vine-sheltered spot,
Linked ever to joys which will ne'er be forgot,
Now mourn in deep solitude; while the winds play
Their dirge-like refrain at the close of each day.

O'er hill-top and valley, o'er meadow and stream,
The dust of his sandals will soon brightly gleam;

And crystals will dance in the fresh morning light,
With diamond lustre as pure and as bright:
While trees will be changed into grand chandeliers,
With pendants created from pure jewelled tears
Which the Ice King shall weep in the cold wintry day
While viewing his palaces wasting away.

In the cool, frosty air, on the smooth window-pane,
Shall beautiful pictures be painted again,
And mosses and ferns in young forests be seen,
Where fairies might gambol the bright leaves between;
Where bowers of crystal shall sparkle like dew,
And blossoms of pearl shall delight us anew;
While garlands, all gleaming with silvery light,
Encircled with beauty, shall ravish the sight.

Yes, winter is coming: and sleigh-bells will chime
With glad, merry voices at bright evening-time;
And the song of the skaters, both youthful and fair,
Shall strengthen the echoes which rend the cool air;
While coasters glide down the crystalline steep,
Delighting to sail o'er the pure wavy deep
Which covers the meadows and valleys like foam,
Congealed, for the pleasure of schoolboys at home.

But round glowing fires happy circles will meet,
Rejoicing once more loved companions to greet,
Where friendship's appeal shall not be in vain,
And the words of pure love shall be spoken again;

While each shall be blest in the welfare of others,
And unity bind closer sisters and brothers,
While with wine of contentment the pure goblets foam,
As each shall recount the true pleasures of home.

Cold winter is coming! Oh, think of the poor
When the Storm Spirit rages around your own door!
Then think of the homeless and heart-stricken one
Who finds no warm hearth, — in the wide world alone.
Then God will reward you with infinite peace,
And your measure of happiness grandly increase;
For 'tis through our acts we the Father adore,
Who leaves to our mercy the outcast and poor.

TO ANNETTE ON HER BIRTHDAY.

ONCE more as the Sun, with his rose-tinted fingers,
Opes wide his blue portals on time, which still lingers,
I think of thy birthday, — a porter still keeping
A watch for its dawning, for joy or for weeping.

A few gentle summers have bloomed for thee here,
Like dewdrops, all glistening life's morning to cheer:
Youth's roses may fade, and its beauties decay,
But a jewel enshrined in its casket will stay.

Though shade amid sunshine may ofttimes steal on,
Obscuring the peace which thy virtues have won;
Though sorrows may sometimes encompass thy way, —
Glad spirits will banish all dark clouds away.

This life is a garden, where flowers oft bloom
But to drop their bright petals like tears o'er our tomb:
Sweet bonds may be severed, and friends may depart,
But memory's signet will live in the heart.

As the glistening stars, those bright gems of the night,
Gain their radiant glow from the great source of light,

Even so may thy virtues conspicuously shine,
With a glow that shall borrow a lustre divine.

Raise thy standard on high with its blazonry bright;
Be valiant with those who have fought the good fight:
Then angels shall guide, through sorrow and strife,
To the conqueror's crown in the temple of life.

THEN LET ME HEAR OF HEAVEN.

When clouds of sorrow, like a veil,
  Obscure life's sunniest skies;
When boisterous winds my bark assail;
  When angry waves arise;
When tossed amid the dashing foam,
  My hopes are almost riven;
When crested billows speed me home, —
  Then let me hear of heaven.

When sailing smoothly o'er the tide,
  With all things bright above,
With chosen friends fast by my side,
  Whose hearts are warm with love;
When Fortune pours with bounteous hand,
  And gifts most sweet are given,
When pleasures come at my command, —
  Then let me hear of heaven.

When comes the twilight of my days,
  Where light and darkness blend,
Then may I catch those glorious rays
  Towards which my footsteps tend;

And when life's golden sands are few;
  When close the gates of even;
When to earth's scenes I bid adieu, —
  Then let me hear of heaven.

When, free from every earthly ill,
  We gain the heavenly shore,
Eternal peace our hearts to fill,
  Increasing evermore, —
Sweet rest within the pearly gates
  And joy supernal given,
There for the weary soul awaits
  The crowning bliss of heaven.

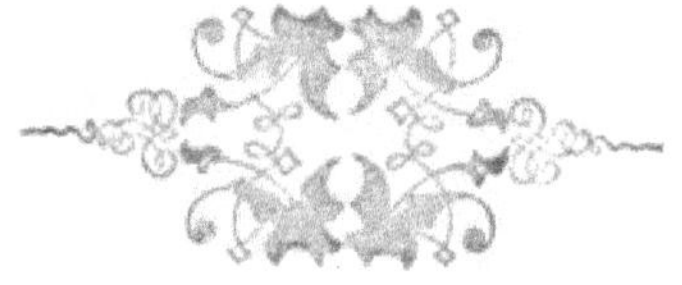

SNOW-FLAKES.

STILL falling, falling, falling fast,
These messengers have come at last,
Descending through the chilly air,
On softest pinions white and fair,
Each like a dove with downy breast
High fluttering o'er its icy nest.

Upon the pinions of the blast,
The tiny flakes rush wide and fast,
Shutting the earth at winter's night
Beneath its coverlet of white,
Keeping the germs secure and warm
From the rude frost and chilling storm.

So coming, coming, coming still
From heaven above, rich blessings fill
Life's chalices with many a joy,
Which time's cold hand can ne'er destroy,
So pure, so holy at their birth,
They sweetly charm the ills of earth.

So, gathered round our toilsome way,
May angel footsteps long delay,
To cheer a weary, burdened heart,
And bid the saddest clouds depart, —
To cause the soul, in hours of night,
Behold the gleams of heavenly light!

Upon my heart, when lone and still,
As freely may pure gifts distil,
Awakening strains of perfect peace,
Whose melody shall never cease,
Till, far beyond the reach of time,
They swell heaven's harmony sublime.

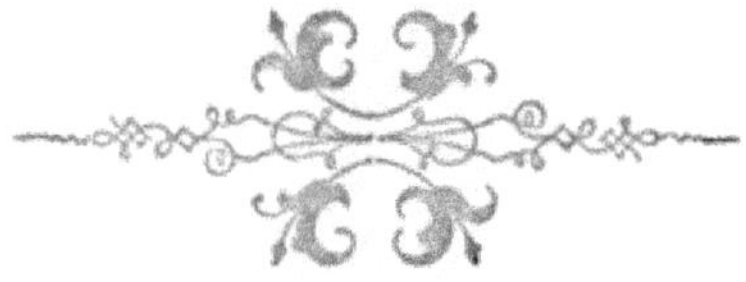

NO, NEVER GIVE UP.

No, never give up while the land is in view;
  Though stormy thy passage through life,
Though meagre thy fortune, though comforts be few,
  Endure to the end of the strife.

No, never give up for the sake of repose,
  Though conflicts be sometimes severe:
No rest to his spirit the warrior knows
  Till victory banishes fear.

No, never give up, though oft cheerless earth seem,
  Though storms of affliction may rise;
For soon heaven's bright day with its glory shall gleam,
  Revealing blest scenes to thine eyes.

No, never give up to thy foe on the field,
  Though valiant and strong be his arm:
The enemy soon to the Christian must yield,
  Protected through grace from all harm.

No, never give up, though the contest be long:
  Thy cause is the cause of the free.
Fight manfully, boldly: then sweeter thy song,
  Then brighter thy laurels will be.

Thy Saviour shall aid thee in time of distress,
  And angels administer cheer:
If courage should fail thee when troubles oppress,
  Then help shall be specially near.

Then never give up; for the land is in view:
  Life's voyaging will shortly be o'er.
A haven of rest with the faithful and true
  Shall be joyfully thine evermore.

THE TWIN SPIRITS.

WHEN Morn with rosy fingers first
  Her portals opened wide, —
Through which the messengers of light
  On golden pinions glide, —
Within the shining band there came
  Two angel forms unseen,
Commissioned o'er the earth to roam,
  Each like a fairy queen.

On dewy pavements air and pure,
  As on a jewelled sea,
With noiseless steps, in sandals light,
  They danced in sportive glee.
Ere long into the heart they flew,
  And claimed the dwelling fair,
Before deceit its walls had stained,
  Or sin had trespassed there.

With lips of purity and truth
  They speak of heavenly things,
And precious treasures ever bear
  Upon their burdened wings.

Around the brow of innocence
  A fragrant wreath they twine,
Upon whose leaves the dews of peace
  Like brilliant jewels shine.

They set their seal upon each heart,
  And lock blest secrets there,
Where sweetest memories lay concealed,
  As in a casket fair.
With kindly words they charm the ear,
  Which breathe of peace and love,
And scatter perfume in their way,
  Which tenderest thoughts can move.

When deep affliction wounds the heart
  Oppressed with pains and cares,
Then Peace extracts the stinging thorn,
  And choicest balm prepares.
She strikes one note upon her lyre
  No other voice can sing,
Which makes responses in the heart
  Of sweetest echoing.

As sisters fair, joined hand in hand,
  They pause at Mercy's gate;
And where Contentment spreads her board,
  They at her table wait.
Sweet flowers bloom along their way,
  With every charm replete,
Which cause full many a heart to bow
  In homage at their feet.

Upon her tranquil, queenly brow
  Peace plants an olive wreath,
And in her sparkling eyes reveals
  A well of joy beneath.
Love, with a winning, dimpled smile,
  Twines garlands round her head,
And weaves within the myrtle boughs
  The roses white and red.

Peace offers with a generous hand
  Her precious treasures fair,
And counsels with a gracious voice
  Most welcome everywhere.
With blushing face and quiet step
  Love plays a modest part;
And, when a citadel is gained,
  She proves her magic art.

Within my breast, as guardian friends,
  May they content abide,
To solace me with words of bliss
  From morn till eventide!
And when the lamp of life burns low,
  And dimly lights my way,
To cheer me in my homeward path
  May these blest spirits stay!

AUTUMN WINDS.

AUTUMNAL winds with plaintive strains
  Disturb the trembling trees,
Which welcomed on the verdant plain
  Each gentle summer breeze ;
For blushes o'er them slowly steal,
  When their cold breath comes near,
Which all their wounded pride reveal,
  But still to us as dear.

As the low murmurs float along
  O'er meadow, field, and wood,
Each bears the burden of a song
  In quite a thoughtful mood.
Each tender form then bows its head,
  And weeps bright tears of dew,
Beneath those leafy boughs outspread
  Which once their glory knew.

In each cool wind an undertone
  Long vibrates on the ear,
Which has a cadence all its own,
  Distinct and ever clear,

Which speaks of joys forever fled, —
  Of scenes forever past;
Time's chariot on its course has sped,
  'Neath shadows overcast.

We grieve to part with Nature's pride, —
  Green leaves and fragrant flowers,
Which, like dear friends, grew near our side
  To cheer the summer hours,
— Those halcyon moments gladly spent
  In childhood's rosy dawn, —
Those golden links to memory lent,
  Till life's last sands are gone.

And yet how beautiful they seem
  To court the frosty air!
As if they found, in pleasing dream,
  Some fairy dwelling there,
Whose gentle whispers breathed at night,
  So charm with secret power,
That gorgeous tints speak their delight,
  When dawns the morning hour.

Though hopes may fail like withered leaves,
  And dirge-like music float
Upon the wings of every breeze,
  With many a solemn note;
Yet though the seasons pass away,
  And mark the year's decline,
It nearer brings the perfect day,
  Which makes heaven's glories thine.

MAY.

ONCE more the fragrant breath of spring
  Speaks kindly unto me,
Though emerald twigs and opening buds
  No more with joy I see ;
But well I know a snowy cloud
  Of blossoms decks the trees,
Inviting with mellifluous sweets
  Gay birds and honey-bees.

The dimpled brooks, long held in chains
  By winter's icy hand,
Now speak their joy with native grace,
  Which we may not withstand ;
And flowers nod upon the banks,
  Kissed by the laughing stream,
As if to greet upon its face
  Each golden, sunny beam.

A choral anthem floats along,
  O'er meadow, field, and wood,
Enlivening with melodious strains
  The deepest solitude,

Where violets profusely bloom
  Within each mossy dell,
And woo warm sunshine through the leaves,
  Which speak their praises well.

I love to think of the new life
  Which decks the stately trees,
And list the song they ever sing,
  Fanned by the vernal breeze.
I love to read upon each leaf
  This sacred, precious truth:
Though we must die, there yet remains
  A blest eternal youth.

A genial glow my pulse now thrills
  While musing on the scene;
A holy charm pervades my heart
  With purest thoughts serene:
For in each leaf and opening bud
  A higher life we trace;
Our drooping forms shall be revived,
  And crowned with heavenly grace.

He who now dots the landscape o'er
  With flowers pure and fair
Smiles ever on his children here,
  And makes us all his care;
And when our mission is fulfilled,
  Each earthly fetter riven,
For us within the pearly gates
  Shall bloom a spring in heaven.

ON RECEIVING MY FIRST BOUQUET.

How pleasant are the gifts which come
  From Friendship's loving hands!
They breathe an influence pure and sweet,
  Which all my praise commands.
Like messengers of good, they charm
  My burdened thoughts away,
And bid me muse on brighter scenes,
  Whose beauties ne'er decay.

Methinks I see the welcome beams
  Of sunny, golden light
Play round their tinted velvet leaves,
  To cheer my wondering sight.
Methinks I hear the words they breathe
  In choicest perfumes rise,
— A grateful offering, ever pure, —
  In anthems to the skies.

These spotless lilies white and fair,
  Which in the valley grew,
Proclaim a glory all their own
  Which royalty ne'er knew.

From out their drooping snowy bells
  A sweet tone seems to come, —
A faint vibration of that song
  Which graced their Eden home.

They speak of faith and hope to me,
  Though in an humble sphere,
And bid me trust a Father's hand,
  Which will protect us here ;
For He who makes these fragile forms
  The object of his care
Will surely let me, poor and weak,
  Rejoice his love to share.

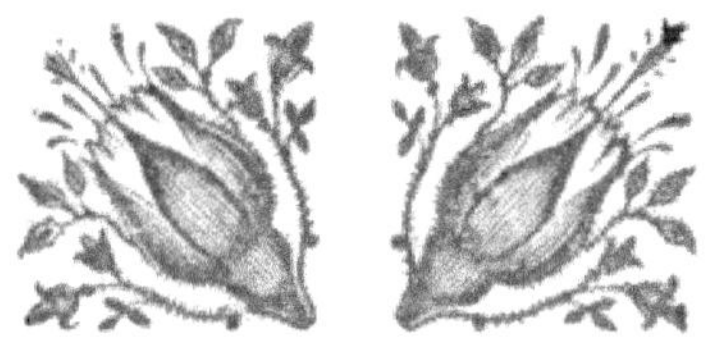

THE CLOVER-BLOSSOM.

"Before the summer was quite over,"
  As fragrant as a flower in May,
I found the little sprig of clover
  Within your note received to-day.
It spoke of one whose heart can tell
  How best to cheer one in distress,
Whose generous deeds I cherish well, —
  May I this simple truth confess?

'Tis but a trifling act to give
  A bud or leaf or smiling flower;
And yet how many kind thoughts live
  Deep in our hearts, born that same hour
When kindly Sympathy extends
  Her genial influence to cheer, —
When smile with heartfelt pity blends,
  So that each word seems doubly dear!

Oh, yes! I knew your "gift was small;"
  But as a "token" true it came,
Which made me many deeds recall
  Which e'er will be unknown to fame:

And yet when in the silent hours
  I number friends and mercies o'er,
Then will sweet buds and scented flowers
  Remind me of thyself the more.

How many a sweet "forget-me-not"
  Is planted in the heart by those
Who think, as from a garden-plot,
  They only bring a blooming rose!
When, nestling in its dewy leaves
  Are fairy children, who can tell
When best to loose their fragrant sheaves,
  In which kind thoughts are treasured well.

FRIENDSHIP'S OFFERING.

"Lilies of the valley" fair,
Objects of your guardian care,
Wet with morning dew,
Bid my muse with pleasure sing,
Bending o'er the offering,
As I think of you.

Strangers from their native beds,
Now they hang their drooping heads,
As I list to hear
What kind messages they bear,
From a heart so free from care,
To my willing ear.

Lurk there here in snowy bell
Fairies who sweet things can tell
To a lonely heart?
Who, with noiseless speech, can bear
Pleasant sounds for me to hear,
Which can joy impart?

On swift pinions, fair and white,
Can they, to my own delight,
Bring me sweet content,
Though but fragrance they convey,
Whispering softly through the day
Words by kindness sent?

Honeysuckles, white and red,
Yield their perfume round my bed
In the days of May,
Culled by thee, that I might know
How the lovely flowers grow
Where the blossoms stay.

Sympathy so good and true,
Ever to the sufferer new,
Here is gladly found;
Breathing out like odors rare,
Filling all the quiet air,
Charming all around.

All good gifts are "from above,"
Messengers of tender love
For our pleasure given;
Redolent with choice perfume,—
Stars which sorrow's night illume,
Winning us to heaven.

Flowers to me are ever dear,
Welcome all the blooming year,
For their sake alone;

But when friendship's hand conveys
Such pure gifts on sunny days,
        Then more prized to own.

May I ever grateful see,
In each kindness shown to me,
        That benignant care
Which adorns the meads and bowers,
Giving sunshine and warm showers
        To the lilies fair!

May I, in my darkened room,
Find true friends to chase the gloom
        With kind words of peace,
Borne to me on lips of flowers,
Till I find in Eden's bowers
        My own sweet release!

SPRING IS COMING.

GENIAL spring once more is coming ;
And the bees will soon be humming
Round the scented thyme :
Now amid the mosses sleeping,
Purple eyes will soon be peeping
In their beauteous prime.

All along the meadows teeming,
Like bright stars in valleys gleaming,
Golden flowers shall bloom,
Welcoming each sunny ray,
Which around their leaves shall play,
And their crowns illume.

Birdlings from the Southern clime,
Glad to hail this pleasant time,
Now in crowds appear,
And in all the forest bowers,
Charming all the morning hours,
Carol sweet and clear.

Flowers fair in meads reposing,
As the wintry months are closing,
Long once more to bloom
With the dewdrops on them lying,
While the morning breeze is sighing
No more o'er their tomb.

Streamlets through green valleys flowing,
All their joy and beauty showing,
Sparkling clear and bright,
Dance along where banks of flowers
Soon shall bless the summer hours
In the warm sunlight.

Fragrance through the soft air stealing,
Unseen treasures fast revealing
From the blooming trees,
Soon shall charm the rosy morning,
Beautified with fresh adorning,
Lading every breeze.

Let all, in these pleasant hours,
Wander in the woodland bowers
In the morning light ;
Seeking health and strength and pleasure,
Thanking God for every treasure
That can cheer the sight.

MY JUNE ROSE.

'Mid the warbling of birds and the breath of sweet
flowers,
Smiling June, like a fairy, has entered her bowers,
With her sandals all sparkling with jewels of light,
Which had crowned sleeping violets through the
still night,
And now scatters her gifts from her bountiful quiver
O'er the emerald banks of our swift-flowing river,
Bidding woodland and meadow and dingle to smile;
While I, as her lover, am happy the while.

A rose deeply blushing she offered to me,
Exhaling its sweetness deliciously free,
Whose velvety petals seemed plainly to say,
"Praise God for pure flowers this bright summer
day:
For his goodness has made us both graceful and sweet,
With purest of pleasures thy senses to greet;
And He who now crowns us with beauty anew
Will surely extend loving care over you.

"Our delicate buds are the work of his hand,
Though unseen, oft we bloom in a lone, distant land;
But our praises in perfume ascend to the skies,
And blessings of dew are his bounteous replies."
So let your heart's offerings freely ascend
To Him who has called himself "Father" and "Friend;"
And He who adorns both the lily and rose,
'Mid showers of blessings, will give thee repose.

Should the Storm King of sorrow and trial pass by,
And clouds of adversity darken thy sky;
Should thy heart bend to earth, as if all hope had fled,
As the rose 'neath the blast bows its beautiful head,—
Then remember the "angel of peace" smiles again;
That sunshine is brighter succeeding the rain;
That the rainbow of hope will soon span the blue sky;
That faith ever triumphs, and love cannot die.

THE OLD SOUTH MILL.

When the day is done and the eve is still,
Is heard the drone of the *Old South Mill*,
Soothing the ear by its monotone,
That the lingerer loves to make his own,
As he leans against the time-worn rail,
While busy thoughts in his mind prevail,
Of times long hid in obscuring mist,
When he hither turned with his yellow grist.

Portsmouth Revisited.

OLD SOUTH MILL.

NIGHT BEFORE DAY.

LIFE has its cares and sadness,
  Its sorrows and its tears:
It knows sweet hours of gladness,
  Imbittered by no fears.

Dark shadows vanish early
  Before the radiant morn,
When dewdrops pure and pearly
  Proclaim fresh beauty born.

Then let not hearts grow weary,
  Nor hope be waning soon;
For morn, though sometimes dreary,
  Precedes a dazzling noon.

OCTOBER.

AUTUMN, with her blushing face,
Greets us now with modest grace,
Like a maid whose heart is stirred
When the voice of love is heard.
Summer's smiles had power to win,
Sunny as it e'er had been,
And bright flowers accorded well
Silently kind thoughts to tell.

Richly dressed in gay attire,
Which must needs our praise inspire ;
Varied with both light and shade,
Like a robe of rainbows made, —
Now she comes, a fairy queen,
O'er the hills and meadows green ;
While on each succeeding day
Steps of beauty mark her way :

Tasselled corn whose golden ears
Glow as her bright car appears,
Glad to feel her magic wand,
As in marshalled ranks they stand ;

While the sheaves of ripening grain,
Scattered o'er the bounteous plain,
Bow their heads with reverent air,
Proud her welcome smiles to share :

Trellised vines along the wall
Quickly heed her gentle call,
And reveal their purple store
Just enough to tempt the more ;
While the orchard's generous pride
Greets her with its juicy tide,
Peeping from a russet screen,
Joying thus to grace the scene.

Could we, like the mountain trees,
Know what words she spoke to these,
As a trembling leaf she kissed
On its bed of amethyst,
We might tell, though high and great,
All must find a lowly state
When earth's pleasures fade away
At the close of life's short day.

Could we know her parting word,
Which the rustling leaflet stirred,
We might tell, though all must die
When death's chilling winds come nigh,
That again in lovelier bloom,
Rising from the silent tomb,
We shall find a glorious home,
Where dread change can never come.

A MINISTERING SPIRIT.

An angel from the realms of light
Once crossed my path in sorrow's night,
Who lingered till the break of day,
Content to wipe my tears away,
And bring blest sunshine to my heart,
Causing the clouds of grief to part.

In earthly garb the "stranger" came,
Unheard her voice, unknown her name;
But there was something in her eye
Which spoke her mission from on high, —
To comfort an afflicted soul,
O'er whom deep billows often roll.

I might have thought her home below,
For thus her form would seem to show;
But as she turned her to depart,
Bequeathing blessings on my heart,
E'en while I mused on heavenly things,
I thought I saw her folded wings.

Sweet memories long linger where
Earth's sunny spots seem bright and fair,
And gratitude our bosoms fill,
Though words be few and thoughts be still ;
But give me sight to plainly see
When angel hands shall wait on me.

12

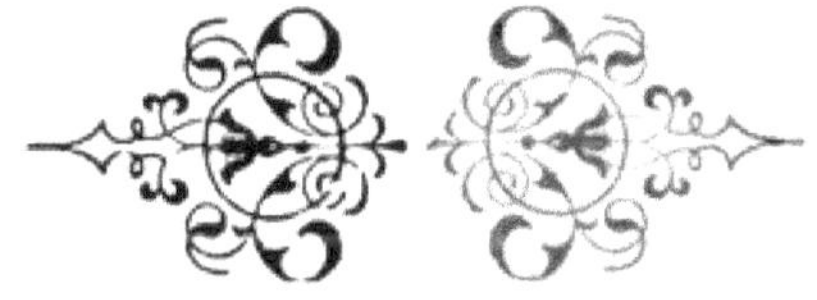

ON A DEWDROP.

Dewdrop trembling in the sun,
  Like a tiny world of light,
Sparkling on thy emerald bed,
  Like a diamond pure and bright,
Let me in thy bosom trace
  Proofs of wisdom, love, and power,
As so skilfully displayed
  In the richly-tinted flower.

Let me view those gorgeous shades
  Playing round thy jewelled form,
Like fair rainbows, azure set,
  When has passed the summer storm.
Into thy clear depths I gaze,
  Seeking out some fairy fair,
Who with magic wand might paint
  Such celestial colors there,

Ocean deep for tiny ships,
  Floating o'er its crystal tide,
Or upon its billows tossed,
  As to distant ports they glide.

Myriads there in silent state,
  Live as 'twere the only home
Where true pleasure did await,
  Or glad sunshine e'er could come.

Myriad stars we o'er us see,
  Sparkling with their mellow light,
Like gems wrought in mystery,
  Dropped by angel hands at night.
Most sublime the prospect is,
  When these distant worlds we view;
But the hand that fashioned them
  Also formed a drop of dew.

THE BREATH OF JUNE.

THROUGH my open casement stealing,
  Comes the breath of bud and bloom, —
Welcome charms to me revealing,
  Redolent with rich perfume.
Summer winds, most softly sighing
  Through the bursting blossoms near,
Bear the whispers of the dying
  To my lonely, listening ear.

Verdant meads, in peace reposing
  By a gently-flowing stream,
When the weary day is closing,
  Charm me like a fairy dream ;
To the evening breeze bequeathing
  Gifts which I would not resign, —
Grateful odors kindly breathing,
  As the twilight hours decline.

Where bright flowers are gayly growing,
  Pleasing every sparkling eye,
There would I, my praise bestowing,
  Joy with them to look on high.

Murmuring woodlands, ever ringing
  With the song of many a bird,
To my solitude are bringing
  Sounds which oft my heart have stirred.

When the lonely hours are dreary,
  And no voice disturbs the gloom,
When distressed and worn and weary,
  Then sweet flowers can cheer my room.
In the stilly night may linger
  By our side some angel form,
Who may write, with magic finger,
  Words which a sad heart may warm.

Oh for those once happy hours
  When my heart and steps were light ;
When I roamed among the flowers,
  Finding there a pure delight !
But these days of pain and sorrow
  Soon will pass with all their gloom :
Soon a blissful, bright to-morrow
  Shall arise beyond the tomb.

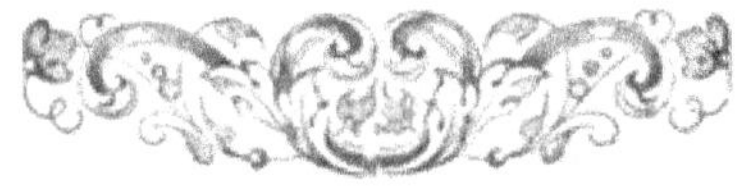

MOONLIGHT EVENINGS.

I LOVE the moonlight evenings,
So beautiful and fair,
When scented leaves and blossoms
Perfume the quiet air:
I love the welcome stillness
These tranquil seasons bring
To care-worn, weary pilgrims,
When time is on the wing.

I love the pleasant moonlight, —
Its silver rays intwined
With golden threads of sunshine,
Which daylight has resigned:
I love the mellow radiance
It scatters all around, —
Its shaded mantle hanging
Where quiet nooks are found.

I love to see the glory
Shine through the veil above,
Spread o'er us like the pinions
Of a protecting dove;

Where, in my steady gazing,
  I think I almost see
Some seraph in his beauty
  With blessing smile on me.

I love these pleasant moments,
  So freely to us given,
When wandering thoughts collected
  May rest intent on heaven ;
When, in a close communion
  With blooming Nature round,
Our hearts' most grateful praises
  Like incense may be found.

Sweet memories always linger
  Around such happy hours,
As welcome to our feelings
  As dewdrops to the flowers.
How often on life's journey
  Bright waymarks we behold,
Where pleasant moonlight evenings
  Can sweetest thoughts unfold!

THE SPRINGING GRASS.

Slowly, surely, still increasing,
  Springs the fresh and tender grass
To fulfil its generous mission
  While the rosy months may pass;
Painting all the lawns and meadows
  With a lovely emerald hue,
Skirting all the murmuring woodlands,
  Which would share its beauty too.

Violets with purple eyelids
  Nestle in the mossy bed,
Peeping out with smiles so winning
  At the azure clouds o'erhead.
Wild-flowers bloom amid the valleys,
  Where the echoing streamlets glide,
Weaving shades within earth's carpet
  Which no artist's hands have dyed.

Beauty reigns all o'er the landscape,
  With her new-born charms replete;
While we gaze with holy feelings,
  As she walks with virgin feet

Through the dells and up the hillsides,
  By the river's sparkling tide,
Dropping flowers to mark her footsteps,
  With the purest thoughts allied.

As the tender grass is springing,
  Silently thus blessing all,
Causing those new charms and pleasures
  Which fond memories must recall,
May that hand that paints the landscape,
  Humbling all man's boasted art,
Write e'en with a golden sunbeam
  Living truths upon our heart!

Casting off the chains that bound them,
  All the tiny buds of spring
Smile to greet the blessed sunshine,
  Which to them new life will bring.
Even so, still patient waiting,
  Gazing upward to the sky,
May we hail that welcome springtime
  Which shall dawn when grief shall die!

OH, SPEAK TO ME KINDLY!

Oh, speak to me kindly!
When through each long and weary day,
Imprisoned in the gloom,
I have no gifts of blooming May,
Of June no sweet perfume,
Then a kind spoken word can soon bring one glad cheer,
Like the sweetest of incense on zephyrs brought near.
Speak to me kindly!

Oh, speak to me gently!
For deep within the heart may lie
The bitter springs of grief,
Which need the light of heaven's fair sky
To bring a sweet relief;
And a kind, gentle word will oft strengthen my heart,
Bidding sorrow and sadness most quickly depart.
Speak to me gently!

Speak cheerfully to me!
When on my burdened spirits fall
Some dark and lowering clouds,

Which with portentous ills appall
In unrelenting crowds,
Then a glad, joyous tone with sweet music can cheer,
Like strains from heaven's own portals brought near.
Speak cheerfully to me!

Speak lovingly to me!
Such holy words fall on my ear,
From lips sincere and true,
As welcome as bright flowers appear
To greet the crystal dew;
For the richest of gifts are the offerings of love,
E'er distilling unseen from their fountain above.
Speak lovingly to me!

Speak hopefully to me!
Oh, tell of rest above the gloom,
Within the heavenly home, —
Of wondrous bliss beyond the tomb,
Where sorrow ne'er can come!
Oh, tell me of beauty, where glories unfold,
Immortal, unchanging, through ages untold!
Speak hopefully to me!

COME TO THE WOODS.

Come with me to the fragrant woods
  When skies are bright and fair,
And, in the depths of their solitudes,
  Forget thy toils and care.

Come stand with me 'neath the whispering pine,
  And gather sweet leaves of fern;
And on the hillocks of green recline,
  And drink from Nature's urn.

Come list with me to the wild bird's notes,
  As to his mate he calls;
While silvery music in silence floats,
  As if in echoing halls.

Sit near the bank of the rippling stream,
  Which gayly glides along
Where golden rays of warm sunshine gleam,
  And dance to the wavelet's song.

Inhale the cooling and perfumed air
  Within the mossy dell,
Where flowerets nestle contented there,
  Their own sweet words to tell.

Commune with Nature, and humbly bow
  Beneath this leafy dome,
And hear the voices she utters now,
  Before thy footsteps roam.

God speaketh by the whispering leaf
  And in the laughing rill,
In perfumes which bright flowers bequeath
  And silently distil.

A "still, small voice" is most distinct
  Within a forest bower,
Which holy thrills of joy can stir
  By their transforming power.

Let all behold the proofs of love
  With warmest gratitude,
And clasp the hand which leads above,
  Mid deepest solitude.

THE MORNING SHOWER.

ONCE more the burning eye of day
Peeps through the gates of morn ;
While lurid beams of mellow light
The lowering skies adorn.

No joyous songs of tuneful birds
Come from the silent woods,
And cooling winds fold up their wings
In deepest solitudes.

No breath disturbs the hanging vines,
Nor stirs the bending grain ;
And drooping flowerets sadly pine
For cool, refreshing rain.

The murmuring streams, with plaintive strains,
The general burden share ;
All Nature seems in silence hushed,
As if in sacred prayer.

The stillness breaks: the fluttering leaves
Proclaim the signs of rain,
And whisper from the topmost boughs
The welcome news again.

The burdened clouds, with generous hand,
Unlock their treasures fast;
And thirsty earth, with parching lips,
Receives the boon at last.

Then smile, with dewy, sparkling eye,
Fair children of the wood;
And dripping lilies bow their heads
With tears of gratitude.

Bright, sunny skies smile lovingly
O'er all the meadows green;
And dimpled brooks and laughing rills
Rejoice to grace the scene.

The emerald twigs are thickly strung
With beads of silver light,
In which a thousand rainbows blend,
And cheer the wondering sight.

Sweet odors from the spicy groves
Pervade the cool, soft air,—
An offering sweet from thousand lips,
Which breathe pure praises there.

High o'er the east, in loveliness,
  The bow of promise bends:
God's signet borne upon the clouds,
  That sweet assurance lends.

So, when dark clouds of sorrow hide
  Life's fairest, sunniest shine,
Let faith, upon the misty veil,
  Behold the hand divine,

"I PITY YOU!"

"I PITY you!" Oh, the sweet, kindly word
Which I in the depths of my great sorrow heard
One weary day!
It fell on my heart like the whisperings of peace,
Whose echoing notes will not speedily cease,
Nor fade away.

Were I estranged from my beautiful home,
Where affectionate words could not speedily come
To cheer my heart;
How would such accents, in sweet, quiet dreams,
Dropped on my ear like bright golden beams,
Bid grief depart!

'Twas a token of friendship, both cheering and good,
To comfort the feeble in deep solitude,
When all alone:
Like sweet music vibrating on memory's ear,
It will cheer me in sadness when trials are near,
When friends have flown.

THE LAST GOOD-BY.

WHEN cherished friends beside us stand,
And warmly grasp the parting hand,
With trembling voice and tearful eye,
We scarce can speak the last "Good-by."

What grief and sadness fill the heart
When with true friends we have to part:
A vacancy so lone and drear
Can but provoke the sorrowing tear.

There is a world forever bright,
Where pleasures bloom in holy light,
Which never with their fragrance bring
Sad ills at last, like thorns, to sting.

There is a land where fadeless flowers
Perpetual grow in sacred bowers,
Whose charms forever give delight,
With nought combined to grieve the sight.

There is a home where angel choirs
Attune their songs to golden lyres;
Where discord's hand has ne'er been given
To rudely sweep the keys of heaven.

There all is perfect, pure, and free, —
All good to seize, no ill to flee;
And every scene new joys shall bring
To make the heart for gladness sing.

There friendship's sweetest bond shall reign
Supreme through all the happy train;
And every voice accord to swell
The praises of Immanuel.

There friends who love may meet again
Beyond the reach of grief and pain:
No parting tears shall dim the eye,
Nor there be heard the last "Good-by."

SUMMER WINDS.

Blow on, ye summer breezes, blow,
  And bring your tribute near,
Which noiseless lips from flowerets kissed
  In sunshine warm and clear;
From laughing rills and pleasant vales,
  Where silvery echoes play,
A cooling freshness bring to me
  To cheer each weary day.

Oh! bear to me an offering sweet,
  Which distant meads withhold,
Which hath a secret power to please
  The youthful and the old.
From dripping leaves and beaded stems,
  From petals fair and bright,
Convey the gifts each would resign
  To cheer my lonely night.

From spotless lilies floating wide
  Upon their native stream,
Whose fairy forms in azure set,
  Like snowy cloudlets seem;

Give me the perfumed words they breathe
  Of purity and love,
When sunny skies serenely fair
  Smile tranquilly above.

Oh! bear to me the gladsome songs
  Of birdlings blithe and gay,
Who wake to hail, in chorus sweet,
  The opening gates of day;
When murmuring woodland, lawn, and stream
  Join in the general strain,
And joy with welcome smiles to greet
  Day's golden car again.

Then still blow on, ye breezes fair,
  And health and joy impart;
Dispense your bounties wide and far,
  And cheer each lonely heart!
May summer winds and birds and flowers
  Proclaim the love and care
Of Him who graciously bestows
  His blessings everywhere!

FADED LEAVES.

THE faded leaves in silence fall,
  Touched by autumnal frost:
Their magic tints are scarcely seen
  Ere they are wholly lost.
E'en so our cherished prospects fail,
  When fairest oft they seem:
Like golden gifts in visions blest,
  They prove an empty dream.

Not all a dream; for life has joys
  And hopes forever dear,—
A wellspring whence delicious streams
  Gush forth most pure and clear;
For in the heart sweet Peace is known,
  And Love attending waits
To catch the faintest whisper there,
  Then opens wide her gates.

The trembling leaves in quiet grew,
  Nor foe nor danger feared,
But drank the sunshine and the dew,
  And smiled when storms appeared.

Thus may I on my homeward path
  Behold heaven's glories nigh,
Nor faint when adverse winds approach,
  When clouds obscure life's sky.

As sentinels with glistening shields,
  The dewy leaves at morn
Announced to blooming nature round
  Another day was born.
Forsaken now, their watch-towers stand
  To mark the place below,
Where troops in scarlet vestures rest,
  Encamped in tents of snow.

Life's springtime smiles with joy and peace,
  And knows few bitter tears :
Its sunny sky, all bright with hope,
  Provokes no gloomy fears ;
But when in grief's desponding night
  The winds of sorrow moan,
Like withered leaves, earth's pleasures seem
  To lie entombed alone.

Above the dead the sighing winds
  Their mournful requiem sing,
Whose plaintive strains to every heart
  The saddest memories bring.
The dearly-loved, the good, the true,
  Like flowers have passed away,
But left the fragrance of their lives
  To cheer us while we stay.

THE BRIEF ANSWER.

I MUSED in silence, and I thought
    Of blessed days to come,
When I in triumph should be brought
    To my eternal home;
Where angels in attendance wait,
    Companions for the blest
Who enter, through the pearly gate,
    The promised land of rest.

I thought of mansions angel-shared,
    With walls of jewelled light;
To which on earth was nought compared,
    So glorious was the sight!—
Of groves and streams and fragrant bowers,
    With every charm replete,
Where Eden's choicest, fairest flowers
    Were clustering round my feet.

I thought of rest—sweet, welcome rest—
    From grief and tears and pain;
Where, with celestial beauty blest,
    To live were joy again.

I saw an angel joyful raise
His censer high in air,
Announcing, with triumphant praise,
That death ne'er entered there.

My heart was stirred with great delight
To greet the blest display
That fell upon my wondering sight.
Oh! must it fade away?
"Can such a home be mine?" I cried:
"Mine such a realm of bliss?"
I paused: "a still, small voice" replied,
And sweetly answered, "Yes."

ON A LILY.

ONCE a fragrant, snowy lily
  Floated down a crystal stream,
Lingering not 'mid scented flowers,
  Where green meads with beauty teem;
Though it sailed through nook so winsome,
  And where dancing sunbeams play,
Yet, refusing e'er to linger,
  Onward still it sped its way.

Though it passed retreats most shady,
  Where the festooned arches hung
To protect from burning sunshine
  Dewdrops hid its leaves among;
Swiftly passing dimpled eddies,
  Dancing o'er the rocks below,
Still intent upon its journey,
  Paused it not their bliss to know.

Onward, onward, still pursuing,
  Gathering strength as on it sped,
Tarried not the snow-white voyager
  Till it found its destined bed

On the breast of heaving ocean,
  Leaping o'er the billowy tide,
Watching e'en with calm composure
  Crested billows by its side.

Even so, pure moral courage,
  Passing down the stream of life,
Deaf to all the world's allurements,
  Pauses not to join the strife ;
Shunning e'en the paths of pleasure,
  Though so harmless they appear,
Beauteous as the modest daisy
  Which adorns the new-born year.

Sailing swiftly down the current,
  With the tempter's power beset,
Lingers not the moral sailor,
  Though life's cup may sparkle yet.
Though the boisterous winds of passion
  Drive him where bright eddies foam,
Still, protected by his armor,
  To his heart no evils come.

Onward still, with strength emboldened,
  Where the path of duty leads,
Soon he finds the golden haven
  Where his honored fame he reads.
Strong to meet all forms of error,
  Which like mists obscure the day,
Safe he rises o'er each billow,
  Chasing grievous ills away.

Conqueror over all temptation,
  Never strong in faith as now,
Virtue her true passport grants him
  By her signet on his brow.
To life's warfare then he marches,
  Like a veteran tried and brave:
Never in the van he falters
  Till he finds a glorious grave.

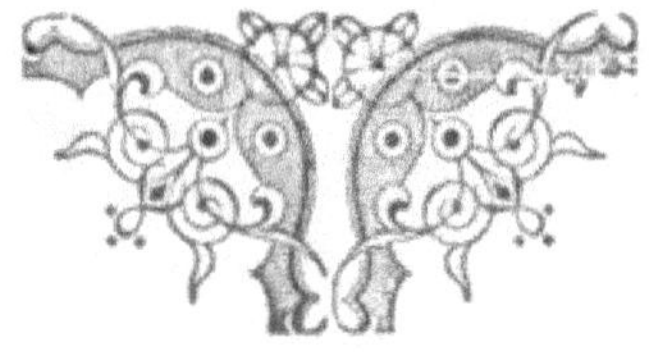

HAPPY MOMENTS.

HAPPY moments, gifts of love,
Angel-visits from above;
Sumptuous feasts in visions bright,
Richest as they take their flight;
Fleeting oft as perfumes sweet,
With their secret charms replete;
Yet they leave fond memories near
To dispel the falling tear.

Happy moments, like those notes
Whose spell on trembling ether floats,
Borne, as from celestial spheres,
To enrapture mortal ears;
Music from an angel's lyre
Purest joys must needs inspire:
Then the soul would fain be free
To swell the lofty harmony.

Happy moments, drops of dew
Gorgeous as each rainbow hue;
Fairest pearls of liquid light,
Dropped by angel hands at night,

As unseen they e'er distil,
And with joy the sad heart fill;
Silently thus charming all
When the shades of sorrow fall.

Happy moments, like the gems
Glittering in diadems;
Yet more pleasing far than they,
Sparkling through life's changing day.
When the soul exulting sings
Of celestial, holy things,
Earthly treasures, though most rare,
Cannot with its joys compare.

Happy moments, stars of night,
Brilliants of celestial light;
Golden beams, from glory given,
Winning us from earth to heaven.
'Mid earth's gloom sweet tidings come
From that better, brighter home,
Bidding us still journey on,
Till the conqueror's crown is won.

THE SPIRIT'S WHISPER.

GRACIOUS Spirit, I would listen
  To thy voice so full of love,
Whispering, in the soul's deep stillness,
  Holy tidings from above.
I would have my heart made ready
  For thy peaceful, quiet rest,
As a dove, with care unwearied,
  Seeketh for herself a nest.

I would cherish thy blest visit,
  When reproof must needs be given,
As kind tokens of God's favor,
  Borne on angel wings from heaven.
I would covet such a guidance,
  Lest my erring footsteps stray;
And would feel thy beams around me,
  Like a sun to light my way.

Whisper to me: tell of glories
  Which adorn the heavenly home,
Where, through grace and faith made perfect,
  Joyous I at length would come.

Let me hear the blessed anthems
  Which pure seraphs love to sing,
To which golden harps in concert
  Sweetest notes forever bring.

Gentle Spirit, whisper to me,
  When in sadness and in tears;
Let the "still, small voice" melodious
  Quick dispel my rising fears.
Onward, then, still homeward tending,
  I may grasp the golden chain
By which blessings pure and holy
  Visit earth like welcome rain.

NATURE'S PAGES.

LET me read from Nature's pages, —
  Truths sublime lie written there ;
Let me find among its records
  Thoughts like jewels passing fair ;
Let me trace the hand of wisdom
  In all things we here behold :
Grove and mountain, stream and fountain
  Each have wonders to unfold.

Forests with their waving shadows,
  Skirted round with grove and lawn,
Tell of silence where, unheeded,
  Beauty blushes with the dawn.
Solitude oft nurtures fancies ;
  But in secret, too, are found
Angel footsteps softly falling,
  So no ear can catch the sound.

Voices 'mid the balmy stillness
  Speak most sweetly to the heart
In pure accents, which, if heeded,
  Bid all gloomy thoughts depart ;

Teaching that in patient waiting
  Strength is gained, though slow our speed:
Towering oaks the storm can battle,
  Zephyrs may uproot the weed.

Mountains, kingly in their grandeur,
  Steadfast point toward loftier skies;
So our souls, by faith made stronger,
  Would unfettered homeward rise.
Upward rising, onward tending,
  With our spirits constant, pure,
May our hopes be firmly rooted
  On foundations strong and sure!

Crystal rivers softly flowing
  Onward towards their goal afar,
Bearing on their azure bosoms
  Fleecy cloud and glistening star,
Speak of Time's swift-gliding current,
  With our blessings mirrored there,—
Royal proofs most kindly given
  Of God's wondrous love and care.

Let me list to Nature's music,
  Sounding o'er her wide domain,
In the purling, rippling current,
  In the soft-descending rain;
Let me hear the rolling thunder
  When the vivid lightnings play;
Feel the glorious Power that guides them,
  Trusting it to guide my way.

Earth is filled with wondrous beauty,
  If but thankful we behold
Treasures easier found and cared for
  Than the world's great idol,—gold.
Costly mines oft lie embedded
  Near our footsteps day by day;
From which pearls of truth are gathered,
  If but patience lead the way.

LINES.

SHOULD darkness o'er thy pathway spread,
And threatening clouds hang o'er thy head,
And trials cause thy heart to mourn,
By deepest sufferings keenly torn,
Then look above, where skies are bright;
Though gloom may intercept the light:
The sun still shines, though hid from view;
And prayer will let the glory through.

For rarest gems most care we show,
On them most labor we bestow,
To find their beauty and their worth,
Hid 'neath their surface from their birth;
So tears and pains, and toils and care,
Are the rough sands oft used to wear
The coarseness from our rougher part,
To show a jewel in the heart.

BUBBLING ECHOES.

ECHOES from the crystal fountain,
  Springing up from depths below,
Pure as on the cloud-capt mountain
  Falls the white and spotless snow;
Let me hear thy liquid music,
  Sounding forth from granite keys;
Touched by fairies' jewelled fingers,
  Sounds sublime but equal these.

Steamlets from the bubbling fountain,
  Gliding on thy steady way,
Let me on thy dimpled surface
  See-the loitering eddies play;
Let me hear the rush of waters
  Foaming o'er thy rocky bed,
Like a white-plumed warrior marching
  Of his loyal troops ahead.

Ocean, to the flowing rivers
  And the living fountains due,
Let me hear triumphant numbers
  Grandly sounding forth from you;

Let me in thy crested billows
  See the jewels sparkle free,
While a thousand rainbows mingle
  With the deep, unfathomed sea.

Echoes from the crystal fountain,
  Speak in silver tones to me
Of pure pleasures gushing upward
  From those depths no eye can see.
Sparkling like thy rippling waters,
  Deeds of virtue I behold,
Dearer to the soul's affections
  Than rare gifts of sordid gold.

Streamlet joyous rushing onward,
  With thy blue lips kissing showers,
Which a bounteous heaven sprinkles
  On thy banks bestrewed with flowers.
Let me, like thy mirrored surface,
  Fully drink of truth and love,
Which, reflected all around me,
  Would in praise return above.

Ocean, deep, deep-sounding ocean!
  In thy depths the type I see
Of that matchless grace which Heaven
  Has most freely shown to me.
May I, like its outspread waters,
  Feel the sunshine of God's love,
Till, on billowy surges, weary,
  Rest I seek like Noah's dove!

Fountain, streamlet, ocean boundless,
  Blend in one harmonious strain,
Echoing back in liquid breathings
  Their pure native tones again;
Let me catch the inspiration,
  Full and pure and free as these;
Let me hear the secret whispers
  Of fair brooks and murmuring trees.

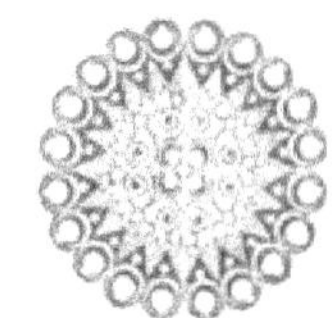

THE OLD ELM.*

I LOVE the old elm in the orchard,
Which slopes to the edge of the stream,
Where, with the fresh spirits of boyhood,
I passed through life's sunniest dream :
Its boughs towered high in their grandeur,
Far up in the fair azure sky,
Where songsters might nestle their offspring,
And mischief could never come nigh.

Its roots, once most firmly embedded,
Were washed by the oft-flowing tide,
Which told to all sorrowing schoolboys,
It might not much longer abide.
We made of its long-running fibres
Some fairy-like baskets at will,
Which earned such acceptable praises
As if wrought with magical skill.

* That graceful elm which formerly adorned the premises of the late Nathaniel Adams, Esq., was removed, in 1844, to make room for the modern improvements in that locality.

SUPPLEMENTARY NOTE.—The editor recalls the scene; but the memory of "Old Jack," the big black dog, obtrudes itself, and mars somewhat the serene picture of the past. Once in the fangs of the beast, and having to jump overboard to save himself, he does not recall the Old Elm as the premium point of his boyhood.—S.

I think of the well-chosen hollow
  In the clean, grassy-carpeted ground,
Where caps filled with apples were carried,
  And desserts for evening were found ;
When, gathered in circles most friendly,
  And cosey as birds in a nest,
We listened to tales oft repeated,
  Exciting each juvenile breast.

How often those tales, which in childhood
  Are mentioned as fanciful things,
Are found in life's warfare more truthful,
  In facts which experience brings !
How oft are those bright, sunny mornings,
  When shadows as strangers are known,
Exchanged for those lone, cheerless evenings,
  When noon into twilight has grown !

Yes : youth has its charms and its pleasures,
  And manhood its joys and its fears ;
Both leaving on memory's tablet
  The well-written record of years.
And while through life's garden we ramble,
  To gather once more its bright flowers,
How often each scene then reminds us
  Of some of our happiest hours !

The elm with its grandeur has fallen,
  A vestige no longer remains ;
The birds have all ceased in its branches
  To sing their melodious strains ;

And the boys who once played in its shadow
  Are scattered wide over the earth,
Denied those exuberant feelings
  Which innocent childhood gave birth.

Although both the elm and the orchard
  Have passed long ago from our sight,
And the hum of the unwearied steam-mill
  Is heard now by day and by night ;
Still round that old spot there yet clusters
  Bright visions of scenes that are past,
And a savor of freshness and gladness,
  Which will ever in memory last.

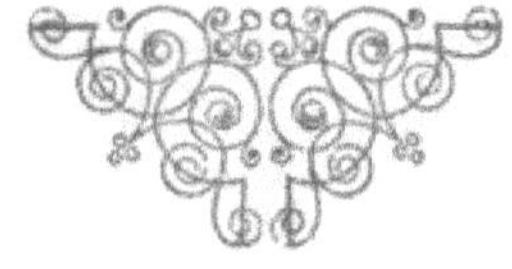

SUNSHINE AND SHADOW.

In pleasant sunshine, warm and bright,
Rich blessings come in golden light,
And fill the heart with joy and peace,
Too pure and holy soon to cease.
Like flowers scattered o'er our way,
Which oft invite a long delay,
They bid us raise our thoughts above
To the sole source of purest love.

When life's young sky is calm and fair,
And silver clouds lie floating there;
When cherished hopes inspire the breast,
Which knows no fears nor sad unrest;
As dewdrops nestle in a rose,
Enjoying there a sweet repose, —
E'en so the soul, content and blest
'Mid sunny smiles, is soothed to rest.

What though a cloud in flowery June
Should yield its crystal waters soon,
And cast a shadow o'er the sky
Just when new glories shone on high!

They only make the scene more fair,
And show us brilliants sparkling there,
Which, blending all in tints most pure,
But make "the promise" still more sure.

When prosperous days, like sunshine, bless
And cheer our souls with soft caress,
Should lengthening shadows darkly come
Around our pleasant, joyous home,
Causing our hearts, with anguish torn
By deepest sufferings, to mourn,
Yet even then bright stars are seen
Emerging with their light serene.

In deep affliction oft are found
Rare gems of truth, though pains abound,
Which only serve to loose the soil,
That else were broke with care and toil;
While living streams of light and love,
Akin to the blest fount above,
Spring forth with consolation sure,
Like priestly incense choice and pure.

In solitude, unseen, unknown,
How oft a weary soul has grown
In heavenly grace, with patient smile,
Though dews of grief fell fast the while!
When trials oft a sad heart fill,
The cup o'erflows with blessings still;
While "ministering spirits" wait
To point the way to Zion's gate.

While homeward still our footsteps tend,
May light and shade together blend,
Uniting in one golden glow,
Which God's eternal love doth show!
Then all within will grow more fair,
No discontent abiding there;
Then all beyond be perfect peace,
Where sorrow, sin, and shadows cease.

SYMPATHY.

How sweetly words of sympathy
  Fall on the sufferer's ear,
Like silvery music heard at night,
  On zephyrs floating near!
They gently calm the troubled breast,
  And bid its tumult cease:
They wake responsive echoes dear,
  Which ever whisper, Peace.

True sympathy, like precious balm,
  Dispels the sorrowing tear,
And bids the clouds of sadness flee,
  With all their shadows drear;
It brings warm sunshine to the heart
  Oppressed with bitter woes,
And soothes the troubled waters fast
  To sweet and calm repose.

It drives the cares of life away,
  Or makes their burden less,
And brings to weary pilgrims oft
  Some gleams of happiness.

Amid the hours of pain and gloom
  'Tis like a star of night,
Which glistens in the dome above
  To make the darkness light.

I treasure up each kindly word
  Or action ever done,
As pictures bright to look upon
  When loving friends have gone ;
And gratefully within my breast
  Shall fondest memories dwell,
Concerning those whose deeds have proved
  Their generous feelings well.

While in these thorny paths I stay,
  While travelling to my home,
I pray that I may often hear
  An angel footstep come
With words of solace to beguile
  A weary hour of pain,
And bid my drooping spirits rise,
  And joy in hope again.

THE SHINING LIGHT.

PILGRIM, on thy heavenly journey,
  Though bright scenes invite delay,
Let not grievous trials turn thee
  From the strait and narrow way.
Look above the clouds that gather,
  Like a curtain dark as night;
Let the golden sunshine rather
  Cheer thee with its welcome light.

Let the glory ever shining
  From the throne e'er guide thy way,
All thy weary steps inclining
  Toward the realms of perfect day.
Let thy thoughts be e'er ascending
  Where thy treasure rests on high;
Gloomy clouds in triumph rending
  By thy faith which cleaves the sky.

Let the dayspring breathing o'er thee,
  With its radiant beams of light,
Keep this precious thought before thee, —
  With God's favor all is bright.

Grief may cast its mantle o'er us,
And dark shadows dim our way;
But the shining light before us
Soon shall chase all gloom away.

May its blissful presence guide thee
— Though the fruits of error lie
With their tempting sweets beside thee —
To thy blessed home on high.
Let the storm then wildly press us,
And dark billows round us roar:
Nought can ever long distress us
While we seek the heavenly shore.

Truth is mighty, and prevaileth,
Like the brilliant sun at noon,
Over unbelief, which raileth
In vain strife to perish soon.
May this holy light beam o'er us,
Like the smiles of God's dear love,
Charming all life's way before us,
Till we reach its fount above!

16

THE DEATH OF THE RIGHTEOUS.

LET me die e'en like the righteous,
  — Strong in faith and full of hope, —
On God's mighty arm relying,
  Confidently looking up.
Let me leave this dreary valley,
  And with angel pinions soar
To the realms of fadeless beauty,
  Where afflictions come no more.

Journeying toward the promised haven,
  Where pure happiness is known,
May I find a Father's welcome,
  And a parent's tender tone!
As the twilight fadeth quickly,
  When the rosy morn appears,
May the glory of his presence
  Soon dispel all lingering fears!

Let me leave this world of sadness,
  Where are known the ways of strife,
And with true, unending gladness
  Enter on that glorious life,

Where long years of pain and sorrow
  Shall be changed to those of bliss;
Where no dreaded, sad to-morrow
  Shrouds our hopes as oft in this.

Let me prize each word so heavenly
  Which the gracious Saviour spoke;
Dearer than the praises uttered
  When the box of ointment broke.
As rare jewels may I cherish
  Each blest promise made for me;
Then my heart can sing for gladness,
  While my faith is strong in thee.

Let me hear the final summons
  For my spirit's glad release,
On my ear enraptured falling,
  As from angels whispering peace.
Let me hear the blessed anthems
  Which the holy angels sing,
Sweetly echoed by the ransomed,
  Who their highest praises bring.

Then, with loved ones gone before us,
  Saved from death and woe and sin,
We, with God's own hand stretched o'er us,
  To his joy shall enter in.
Then our bliss shall be made perfect,
  Throughout ages ever blest;
And eternal glory crown us
  Where the righteous find their rest.

ON A WHITE ROSE

Rose, upon thy fragile stem,
  White e'en like the fleecy snow,
Crystal fount nor sparkling gem
  Can such grateful odor show.
And we prize thee, spotless, pure;
  Like a pet we give thee place:
Though thou mayst not long endure,
  Yet may we a lesson trace.

Innocence and beauty blend
  In thy soft and velvet dress;
While thy blushes likewise tend
  To increase thy loveliness.
Modest grace here, too, we see,
  Couched beneath thy emerald bed:
Till the mild wind kisses thee,
  Hidest thou thy white-crowned head.

So true merit often lies
  Close concealed in modest dress,
And the world's gay pomp denies,
  Choosing with kind deeds to bless.

Like sweet incense kind distilling
  Healthful balm on all around,
Every heart most gladly filling
  With such peace as may abound.

When the winds arise, exciting
  Vines that tremble on the eaves,
Quickly to the call replying,
  She her sweet concealment leaves.
Then her worth is soon discovered,
  And her fame to all is known:
Praises then, as wreaths all fadeless,
  On her head rest like a crown.

Roses droop and fade and wither,
  And their tender petals fall:
Grief the sunniest sky o'ershadows
  When loved friends obey the call;
Bidding them put off their blooming
  When their vigor fades so fast,
And the tomb, so sad and lonely,
  Holds the treasure firm at last.

But dear friends, unlike the flowers
  With celestial beauty blest,
Shall, when sounds the heavenly signal,
  Break their cold and silent rest.
They shall come, made like the angels,
  From all lands, afar and near,
To the home of many mansions,
  Which we hold in hope so dear.

ONE KIND WORD.

One kindly word, how sweet its tone,
When dropped from lips sincere!
It has a cadence all its own,
So soft, so pure, so clear.

The gentlest whisper may convey
Blest music to the heart,
And vibrate through each happy day,
Touched by its magic art.

Sweet memories will gather fast
Around our paths each day,
And peace a golden sunshine cast,
Not soon to fade away.

And, when we cull the choicest flowers
Which bloom to charm us here,
They but recall those halcyon hours
By friendship e'er made dear.

Let loving words fall on my ear
In such bewitching tone,
That I may still sweet music hear
When dearest friends have gone.

Then on some calm and twilight hour,
  When zephyrs fan the trees,
Shall I still feel their cheering power
  When whispered by the breeze.

And when sweet perfumes fill the air
  At morning's rosy hour,
They will but speak of joys most rare,
  Which bloomed in friendship's bower.

No kind, sweet word is e'er forgot,
  Which springs from feelings true:
Each is a bright "Forget-me-not,"
  All wet with sparkling dew.

ON A SLEEPING CHILD.

SLEEP on, thou little slumberer,
  Upon thy mother's arm:
Thou know'st no fear nor sorrow there,
  Secure from all alarm.
In quiet dream thou restest now,
  As on a bed of flowers, —
E'en as a lily bows its head
  When fall the summer showers.

Blest angels guard thy little bed,
  And fold their wings to stay
Beside thy lovely form, to keep
  All shadows far away.
And, when the sunshine's golden lips
  Drink up the dew at dawn,
They plant fair blushes on thy cheeks,
  Caught from the breath of morn.

Sleep on, thou little innocent;
  Enjoy thy peaceful rest,
E'en like a timid, gentle dove
  Within its downy nest;

And when thy merry, happy songs
  Float on the perfumed air,
No liquid note will sound more sweet,
  No silvery chimes more rare.

When through the woods and shady dells
  With buoyant steps you roam,
To cull the sweetest, choicest flowers
  To grace thy native home,
May you with joyous heart behold,
  Upon the petals fair,
The tokens of thy Father's power,
  Who makes us all his care!

And when shall pass away so soon
  Thy childhood's hours serene;
When duty's silent voice shall lead
  Through many a varied scene, —
May benedictions from the skies
  Beam on thy upward way,
Till all earth's cares and griefs are lost
  When dawns the perfect day!

"AS RAIN UPON THE MOWN GRASS."

As on the fragrant, new-mown grass
  Descends the summer rain,
Which bids the drooping flowers revive,
  And smile with joy again ;
So may thy Spirit on our hearts
  Like gentle dews distil,
Imparting to us needed grace
  Our mission to fulfil.

May light and joy and peace be ours,
  Descending from above, —
Those blessed gifts which God doth send
  As tokens of his love !
May their sweet influence give us cheer
  When sunshine fades away,
And bring unto our burdened souls
  The gleams of heavenly day.

AUTUMN.

Autumn, with a queenly beauty,
  Walks in triumph o'er the plain,
Giving to the changing woodland
  All their varied charms again.
As she glides with measured footsteps
  O'er the hills and meadows green,
Every tender leaf is tinted
  Ere her royal robes are seen.

Golden sheaves of bounteous harvest
  Welcome her each sunny morn,
When they hear her rustling garments
  Passing through the fields of corn ;
When with patient ear they listen
  To the words she chants the while,
Which can cause their withered graces
  With a pleasing joy to smile.

In parterre and blooming valley,
  Where the bright flowers lingering stay,
In warm sunshine all rejoicing
  Ere their glory fade away,

She draws near with timid footsteps,
  Lulling all to dewy sleep,
Loving o'er their peaceful slumbers
  Guardian watchfulness to keep.

On the sighing wind she breatheth
  Pensive tones for every year,
As a requiem o'er the lost ones,
  Who performed their mission here.
Like a fragrant bud of summer,
  Drooping when they seem most fair,
Cherished words to us bequeathing,
  Chaining sweetest memories there.

With untaught but skilful fingers,
  She weaves chaplets for the dead
Ere the fading, trembling leaflets
  Seek their lowly, mossy bed;
While in those rare tints she painteth,
  With a true and skilful hand,
Types we see of fadeless beauty,
  Which adorns the better land.

Like the changing leaf of autumn,
  Man must also pass away,
Though the voice of love and friendship
  Loud invite a long delay;
But beyond earth's changing shadows,
  Where its griefs and cares ne'er come,
Scenes of endless joy invite him
  To a blest, eternal home.

MIDDLE STREET CHURCH.

These stanzas, by the late Miss Eliza O. Shores, apply to the present scene. In the Middle Street Church, the lamented Horton D. Walker, Mayor at the gathering in 1853, worshipped :

To scenes, to friends in childhood dear,
In after life we fondly stray ;
But oh, how sad these scenes appear,
When those loved friends have passed away !
With pensive pleasure we renew
Acquaintance with the dreamy past,
And as the picture starts to view,
We wish it would forever last.

"I WISH I WERE A BIRD."

I WISH I were a little bird,
  All beautiful and bright:
My liquid carol sweet and pure
  Should wake the morning light;
When sunbeams chase the shadows fast,
  From flowery vales away,
My matins I would blithely sing
  To charm the early day.

To lonely chambers dark and still,
  Where music ne'er is heard,
My choicest strains I there would sing,
  My heart with pity stirred;
Upon each warm and sunny day,
  Close by the window-seat,
Beneath the leafy bowers oft
  My lay would I repeat.

To those who never joyous see
  The rosy morning light,
My willing tribute should be given
  With most sincere delight.

When weary hours grow long with pain,
  The oftener I would sing,
And try some cheering gift to bring
  Upon my burdened wing.

To lonely hearts all desolate,
  Who find no happy hour,
Nor even in earth's treasures fair
  Can see one beauteous flower,
Would I my tenderest strains oft pour
  Close by their listening ear,
Till to their quickened souls would seem
  An angel's anthem near.

Then shadows now which needless fall
  Upon the lone and weak
Should yield to golden sunshine bright
  Before one fleeting week:
Desponding souls should quickly rise,
  Their hearts with pleasure stirred,
Because they only heard the song
  Of one kind little bird!

THE MORNING COMETH.

THE morning cometh ! sweet the word
  Proclaimed on watchtower's height :
The cheering accent now is heard ;
  Soon ends this dreary night.

For us the sound is kindly given
  To chase our fears away ;
And soon our eyes shall view that heaven
  Where reigns eternal day.

The morning cometh ! echo far
  The welcome tidings, free !
Though night may boast full many a star,
  The sun must rise for thee.

The morning cometh ! joyful note !
  How blissful is the sound !
On fragrant breezes may it float
  This groaning earth around !

Let every captive lend an ear
  Who toils beneath his load;
Let every soul the message hear,
  And choose the heavenly road!

As oft our highest joys we gain
  Through grief and bitter tears;
So dreary night on earth must reign
  Before the morn appears.

But sin has reigned a tyrant long,
  And we have felt its power:
Its gloomy bands, though forged and strong,
  Must vanish in an hour.

How great the change, when day shall gleam,
  Perpetual, glorious, bright!
An emblem fair each ray will seem
  Of beauty and delight.

Thy warfare, Christian, soon will end;
  Thy race will soon be o'er;
God will thy constant peace defend
  Where tears shall fall no more.

The morning cometh! saints, rejoice!
  The "dead in Christ" shall rise,
And welcome with angelic voice
  Their Saviour in the skies!

Redeemed from all that can destroy
  Their holy, heavenly peace,
Pure praises shall their songs employ,
  Their transport never cease.

Haste, Lord, that promised glorious morn!
  Attend thy children's cry!
And let refulgent glory dawn
  Across the eastern sky!

Confirm our hopes, entrance our eyes,
  With but a glimpse of thee!
Then would our ransomed bodies rise
  When we thy face shall see!

Enraptured with thy presence, Lord,
  We at thy feet would fall,
And feast delighted on each word,
  And claim thee "all in all."

But patiently we still would wait
  Till thine own time hath run:
Then through thy mercy, free and great,
  The "victory" will be won!

THE SUMMER RAIN

ON trembling leaves and opening buds
  The bounteous rain descends,
And with soft murmurs through the woods
  Sweet, pensive music blends.

The meadows, lawns, and lovely vales,
  In livelier robes are seen
To smile content on all around,
  And boast their fairy sheen.

Those flowers which languished on the plain,
  And hung their drooping head,
Now with a conscious vigor bloom,
  With brighter leaves outspread.

The little rill which slowly ran
  Adown the sloping hill,
Now quicker speeds its headlong course,
  Its mission to fulfil.

The trees a cooling freshness give
  To the soft, balmy air;
While sunny skies through fleecy clouds
  Smile on the prospect fair.

The bubbling brooks now quickly pour
  Their well-filled stores along,
To do their office at the mill,
  And swell the laborers' song.

The violets on their tender stems
  Receive the precious boon
Which bounteous Heaven thus kind bestows,
  Lest they should fail too soon.

Fresh roses ope their petals wide
  To drink the blessing rare;
While dewdrops linger on their stems,
  As pure as diamonds are.

Fair daisies on the mossy banks
  With purest light are crowned;
While silver leaves and beaded twigs
  On every hand are found.

So let created Nature boast
  To show a fairer face,
And open new her fruitful stores
  In every lovely face.

CONSOLING PROMISE.

"And God shall wipe away all tears from their eyes; and there shall be no more death, neither sorrow nor crying, neither shall there be any more pain: for the former things are passed away." — REV. xxi. 4.

THRICE happy that expected day
  When sorrows shall be o'er,
When earth-born trials flee away,
  And tears be shed no more!

While here we dwell, though blessings flow
  Profusely in our way,
And on our hearts their charms bestow
  Throughout life's fleeting day, —

Yet troubles, like the thorn, oft spring
  To mar our transient joy,
And unseen evils sadly bring,
  Which cause us more annoy.

No constant, true, abiding peace
  Is promised long below;
Nor will our souls find sweet release
  While sin remains our foe.

Nor is there one confiding soul,
  Whate'er his joys may be,
Who can his destiny control,
  And bid all sorrows flee.

Through tribulation's thorny way,
  The gate is often found
To those blest scenes, where angels stay
  And feast on holy ground.

There Christians find, with humble hearts,
  Sweet converse with their Lord,
And learn, what nought but grace imparts,
  True knowledge of his word.

Christ, the Forerunner for our good,
  Victorious led the way,
Through gloomy sorrow's dismal flood,
  To realms of brighter day.

He felt the world's opposing scorn,
  Its bigoted disdain;
With grief he wandered, oft forlorn,
  And suffered every pain.

If then, as "children," we obey
  His ever-gracious voice,
He soon will wipe our tears away,
  And bid us e'er rejoice.

We then shall share his constant love,
  Exempt from every pain,
And all enrapturing pleasures prove, —
  A great eternal gain.

A "recompense" we then shall find
  For every earthly ill,
And know in truth that God designed
  His glory to fulfil.

Faith, grace, and patience, Lord, impart
  To each afflicted here,
That he may wait with cheerful heart
  Till thou, his hope, appear.

PARTING WITH CHRISTIAN FRIENDS.

When with dear friends we have to part,
What chilling sadness fills the heart!
Too deep for tears or sighs to show,
And only felt by those who know
The bonds of love which God has given
On earth to be confirmed in heaven.

If such affection, then, may wait
In those who dare anticipate
An heirship to the heavenly throne,
— A glorious kingdom for their own, —
How sad the last kind words appear!
How doubly sad the silent tear!

No parting word will need be given
By those who share the bliss of heaven,
Nor absence ever be deplored
When Eden blest shall be restored.
But, in each other's presence blest,
Our happy souls will find sweet rest.

Oh! let the glorious day draw nigh
When every fear and every sigh,

When every farewell tear shall cease,
Our hearts enjoy perpetual peace.
Then on the promised heavenly shore
Our songs of praise shall fail no more.

Soon may we, on fair Salem's ground,
With all the ransomed throng be found,
With them to view the better land,
Richly adorned by God's own hand,
With crystal streams and valleys bright,
And all things which can give delight.

Victorious over every foe,
No more shall they sad bondage know:
Their peace no cares shall e'er annoy,
Their cheering hopes no power destroy;
Transcendent joys shall e'er await
Each soul that enters Zion's gate.

No doubt one pang shall e'er afford
The soul reposing in the Lord:
Each wondrous scene shall then conspire
To keep alive the holy fire,
Uniting hearts in perfect love,
Enduring as the throne above.

CONFIDENCE IN GOD.

"Behold, as the eyes of servants look unto the hand of their masters, and as the eyes of a maiden unto the hand of her mistress; so our eyes wait upon the Lord our God, until that he have mercy upon us." —Ps. cxxiii. 2.

As servants watch their master's hand
  To know his fondest will,
So would we wait at thy command,
  Each mandate to fulfil.

Not with a dread and slavish fear
  Would we thus seek thy face:
Our waiting souls would *gladly* hear
  Thy messages of grace.

We ask for mercy, and our eyes
  Look for a sign from thee.
The gift is free: thou bid'st us rise,
  And all our sorrows flee.

E'er watchful for the Spirit's voice,
  We would each call obey:
To do thy will would be our choice,
  Our chief delight each day.

Thy promise makes our tasks most light,
  Thy counsels give us joy;
And every day seems always bright
  When spent in thy employ.

Prostrate before our Master's feet,
  Submissive to his will,
We gladly stay, and love to meet
  To keep his precepts still.

He feeds our longing souls anew,
  He gives us angels' food:
The great supply he bids us view,
  And leave inferior good.

We wait and feast, like friends we fare:
  No strangers here abide;
His humble followers subjects are,
  Who tarry at his side.

As "sons" he greets them, kindred dear;
  No aliens here are known;
As servants they no more appear,
  Their birthright now is shown.

Approved as "children," we would share
  Our Father's smiles below,
That soon with triumph we may wear
  That crown he will bestow.

STILL HOPE FOR THE BEST.

THE morn of thy life may prove sunny and clear,
And prospects grow brighter with each rolling year;
Sweet flowers may smile all thy pathway along,
And hearts tuned in concert respond to thy song;
Rejoice in thy pleasures with innocence blest,
Remember thy mercies: still hope for the best.

The day still advancing, each hour may prove
Thy noon the enjoyment of faith and of love;
And hope, with its brilliant and beautiful rays,
May lighten thy path, and give peace to thy days:
In all things give thanks, with contentment e'er blest,
Forget not thy weakness: still hope for the best.

The shadow declining, dark clouds may arise,
And tears of deep anguish may flow from thine eyes;
The bramble may flourish where roses once grew,
And enemies boast where kind friends were once true:
Though thy heart may despond, by sad trials oppress,
Faint not, nor be weary: still hope for the best.

Though earth may look dreary, and darkness surround
Those scenes where we hoped joy and peace would be found,
And kindness and sympathy fail to bestow
That comfort the sufferer most wishes below:
Though thy days pass in gloom, by drear bondage distrest,
Yet trust to the future: still hope for the best.

Thy pilgrimage, Christian, will soon have an end;
Angel-guards even now on thy footsteps attend,
To guide thee through dangers unseen on thy way,
To comfort, to strengthen, to cheer thee each day.
Endure, then, thy conflicts; for soon thou shalt rest.
The conquest is certain: still hope for the best.

The tried sons of Zion will shortly come forth
From east and from west, from south and from north,
To claim in those mansions of glory above
That abode where shall reign the perfection of love.
The warfare accomplished, the saints then shall rest,
Forever triumphant: then, hope for the best.

I AM WEARY OF STAYING.

I AM weary of staying: oh! soon let me rest
In that beautiful land which is made for the blest;
Let me dwell in those mansions of glory and light,
Where pleasures untold shall my sorrows requite.

I am weary of staying: oh! let my pains cease;
Let my spirit from bondage obtain its release;
Let me revel forever in blessed repose,
With that ecstatic bliss which the pure seraph knows.

I am weary of earth, and I wish to go home;
For where lies my treasure no evils can come;
Though bright scenes are here found, which invite my
delay,
A future more glorious forbids me to stay.

I am weary of staying alone in thick gloom,
Like a prisoner in darkness as still as the tomb;
Bereft of warm sunshine, which gladdens the day, —
Of the moon's silver beams, which chase shadows
away.

"THY WORD, O GOD! IS PURE."

THY precious word, O Lord! is pure,
  Thy precepts just and right:
Thy promises, forever sure,
  Shine forth with holy light.
Like diamonds scattered by our way,
  They lure our footsteps on:
We gain new treasures day by day,
  Till life's last goal is won.

Gifts from thy precious, bounteous store
  Must need be wise and good:
We taste, and gladly ask for more;
  We feast on angels' food.
Still let us from the fountain drink
  Of living waters pure;
Then faith will never let us sink,
  But peace and strength secure.

"A lamp" to guide our erring feet,
  "A light" to cheer our way,
Such signals are most truly meet
  To guard us lest we stray.

Still let the truth more brightly shine
  Amid surrounding gloom ;
And, when life's hopes and joys decline,
  Safe light us through the tomb.

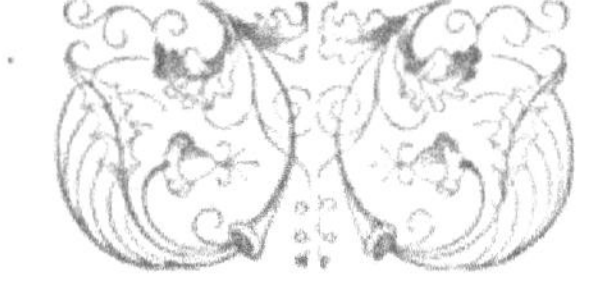

TO "BIRDIE" D.

One morning when the skies were fair,
And clover-blooms perfumed the air,
    When hill and dell and wood and lawn
    Rejoiced to hail the beauteous dawn,
An angel at the portal stood
That guarded my dark solitude ;
    And voices called, that I might see
    The vision which awaited me.

Not quite an angel ; for I knew
That golden hair and eyes of blue,
    And dimpled cheeks, and coral lips,
    Sweet as the dew a fairy sips,
Proclaimed her of a mortal birth, —
A precious floweret of the earth,
    Who could no song of seraph sing,
    While folded lay an angel wing.

Dear child, in thy sweet, winning face
The lines of goodness all can trace :
    Thy generous heart full well we know
    Will oft thy little all bestow,

If but thy playmates, too, may share
The good things, which thou think'st most rare ;
Thy peace and joy gild every smile,
And trilling laughter charms meanwhile.

May thy young life forever be
Pure as the love which guardeth thee !
No tears bedim thy laughing eyes,
No cloud obscure thy sunny skies ;
And when you view heaven's pearly gate,
Where for your coming angels wait,
Then, spotless, with no stain of sin,
Unfold your wings and enter in.

AFFLICTIONS.

AFFLICTIONS sent by God's command
  Are messengers of love:
They bid us view the chastening hand,
  And set our hearts above.

They bid us leave our wandering ways,
  Our all in him confide,
That we may all our future days
  In constant trust abide.

'Tis thus the Father shows his care
  For all his sons below;
For no true blessings would he spare
  To save from death and woe.

He seeks our good, our greatest peace,
  And unknown bliss intends;
He bids from sinful pleasures cease,
  And take the gifts he sends.

Though present hopes and comforts flee
  Like early dew away,
Far greater joys we soon shall see,
  When dawns the promised day.

Eternal peace and joy shall crown
  Each humble, contrite heart:
God will with love each soul surround,
  And bid all grief depart.

HYMN.

O GLORIOUS day of heavenly rest!
  We hail each sign of thee:
With eager hearts and longing eyes,
  We wait thy dawn to see.
Those gilded rays of glorious light,
  Resplendent as the sun,
Must soon to every eye make known
  The holy coming One.

With cheerful hope and earnest prayers,
  Still trusting in thy word,
We long to see the eastern skies
  Reveal thine advent, Lord!
Then would our waiting souls rejoice,
  Could we thy face behold:
In ages of triumphant bliss,
  Our joy could ne'er be told.

O blissful day of promise blest!
  We long to share thy peace,
When pain and every ill shall end,
  And pleasures never cease;

When rapturous joy, like holy fire,
  Shall swell our song of praise,
And every wondering, grateful heart
  Shall cheerful accents raise.

Redeemed beyond the reach of sin,
  Victorious o'er the grave,
The ransomed shall with angel tongues
  Adore thy power to save.
To golden lyres each voice shall tune
  An anthem sweet and strong:
"To Christ, who saved us by his blood,
  All glory shall belong."

O glorious day! with haste draw near;
  For we would share thy rest:
We long, from every evil freed,
  To be supremely blest.
Oh! shed thy beams of glory forth,
  Dispel this gloomy night,
And let the earth, renewed, rejoice
  To see thy welcome light.

19

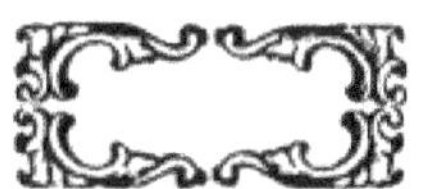

A SPRING MORNING.

How cheering to the careworn heart
  To view the gladsome spring!
When Nature in sweet harmony
  Can her new anthems sing.

The Earth, so long in ermine dressed,
  Puts on her robes of green,
That she may, in her fresh attire,
  Now grace a lovelier scene.

Gay flowers bloom along the way
  In which we thoughtful roam,
And charm our eyes with visions bright,
  Foretelling scenes to come.

The warbling birds on every tree
  Attune their little throats,
And stir sweet chords in every heart
  Which lists their welcome notes.

Refreshing odors fill the air
  From all the blooming trees,
Which freely yield their perfumed gifts
  To the soft-whispering breeze.

Let man awake, and view such scenes,
  Which free to all are given,
Nor lose in drowsy hours such joys, —
  The kindly gifts of Heaven.

'Tis for the happiness of all
  That birds with soaring wing
Their anthems pour in accents pure,
  Their sweetest tributes bring.

'Tis for the eye of every one
  The fields and fragrant bowers
Are in their richest garments dressed,
  To charm such holy hours.

Then let us all these gifts enjoy
  With cheerful gratitude,
And warmly praise their Maker, God,
  In accents oft renewed.

I LONG TO GO HOME.

I LONG to go home ; for too long I delay
In a strange foreign land, where, by night and by day,
Temptations most grievous my progress withstand,
As onward I haste to the beautiful land.

I long to go home ; for I gladly would rest
From evils by which I have long been distrest :
As a stranger and pilgrim, I look with delight
For the end of my journey with prospects most bright.

I long to go home ; for I would not delay
To add to my march but the length of a day :
The glimpse I have had of that glorious land
Makes me eager amid all its beauties to stand.

The night is far spent with its sorrows and fears,
Where strength has been gained amid trials and tears :
The day is just breaking, — the sun I behold
Through fair shining portals its glories unfold.

The cloudlets of grief here no longer stay,
As his bright, shining arrows chase darkness away:
My mind's sky is clear, like a rose-tinted morn,
When flowers look upward where beauty is born.

I long to ascend to my dear Father's home,
Where his children, all gathered, with transport shall
come;
With hearts firm united by love's blissful chain,
Whose links death can never dissever again.

I rise on the pinions of faith like a dove
Bound homeward to carry its message of love:
I gaze on the prize as it glistens afar,
Encircled with light, as a true guiding star.

I eagerly long that blest country to see,
Where glorified spirits are waiting for me,
And meet with those loved ones, who, little before,
Passed gently away to the heavenly shore.

Already there falls on my glad, listening ear,
Pure anthems celestial, most welcome to hear;
And I long to be swelling the chorus sublime
Which shall echo, as now, through the portals of time.

My journey is ending; and almost at home
I hear angel voices, like blest spirits, come
To beckon me on to that heavenly rest,
Where all trouble shall end, and the weary are blest.

CHRISTIAN PILGRIM'S EXPECTATION.

While dark and ever-changing scenes
Beset the weary pilgrim's way,
How joyful does he hail the gleams
Of heavenly, light-bespeaking day.

When in deep trials oft he meets
With sad affliction's withering hand,
His burdened soul with rapture greets
Each token of the promised land.

By faith he views his sufferings o'er,
And all his weary wanderings cease ;
While prospects brightening more and more
Shall welcome him to endless peace.

Fair Eden's bowers appear in bloom,
Which blossom ne'er to fade away ;
Whose tinted flowers of rich perfume
Shall live throughout eternal day.

No "pricking brier nor grieving thorn"
  Shall more afflict fair Zion's sons;
The sacred, blest, sabbatic morn
  Shall bring release to ransomed ones.

All tears will then be wiped away,
  Sickness and death, their sorrow o'er,
Angelic beauty ne'er decay,
    And gladness reign forevermore.

Then shall the earth renewed rejoice
  That "former things" have passed away,
And groaning Nature's stifled voice
  Shall hail the long-expected day.

In expectation still we wait
  For Zion's coming to be known;
When saints shall claim their priestly state,
  And Christ shall reign on David's throne.

BE STEADFAST.

Be steadfast when faith soars majestic and free,
And gains the blest world of delight,
When carnal allurements and temptations flee,
And earth fades away from the sight.

Then hope, like an anchor, holds steady and sure,
Though tempests and storms may arise :
The passage is certain, the harbor secure,
The prospect, how blest to our eyes !

Be steadfast ! though darkness prevails o'er thy way,
Though grieved in adversity's night.
Behind the dark curtain which hides thee from day,
Are regions of heavenly light.

Though doubts may oppress thee, and cause thee to fear,
"Be steadfast," and "hope to the end :"
When deepest thy sorrows, then Jesus is near,
With promise and grace to defend.

THE VOICE OF THE SHEPHERD.

THE voice of the Shepherd speaks kindly to me,
Though in the thick darkness no image I see:
His accents are laden with mercy and love,
Melodiously sweet as the music above.

When in the dark valley of sadness I roam,
Afflicted, desponding, away from my home,
I list 'mid the stillness those glad tones to hear,
Which strengthens my heart, and dispels every fear.

While here a lone traveller 'mid sorrows and fears,
Whose burden is known by the measure of years,
A message most welcome is whispered to me,
"The King in his beauty" thine own eye shall see.

What though fairest flowers are now hid from my view,
And meadows all sparkling with pure crystal dew,
Or beautiful landscapes, afford no delight,
Their multiplied charms all veiled from my sight!

What though gorgeous sunsets fade slowly away,
Like the kind parting smile of a fair summer day,
And the curtains of night overshadow the earth,
Embroidered with gems, as when first it had birth!

'Tis not for my joy that the bright sunshine gleams,
Nor the moon's silver lips kiss the valleys and streams;
But in the deep silence my faith can behold
The home of the blest, where new beauties unfold.

In that fair "better land," where the ransomed shall
dwell,
Shall new glories celestial all shadows dispel,
And the voice of the Shepherd enrapture the soul,
While ages on ages unceasingly roll.

THE SOUL'S ANCHOR.

Our life is like the changing sea,
  Whose foaming billows rise and fall
Obedient to the great decree
  Which governs all things great and small.

But though its surges high may roll,
  And wildly toss our trembling bark,
Yet hope, the anchor of the soul,
  Shall hold us safe, though night be dark.

That power which rules the raging sea,
  And bids the waves in quiet sleep,
Shall quickly make all shadows flee ;
  While holy angels near us keep.

His love shall cheer our roughest way
  When to our hearts no joy appears ;
Imparting comfort day by day,
  Which soon dispels foreboding fears.

When trials, like thick clouds, arise
  In gloomy sorrow's dismal night,
And darken e'en our happiest skies,
  When life's bright star would shine most bright,

Still trusting to our pilot sure,
  We eager watch the dawn of day,
When heavenly light, with rays most pure,
  Shall chase all shadows far away.

In sailing o'er life's trackless main,
  Where golden sunbeams peaceful play,
As if with gems at home again,
  Which sparkle through the livelong day,

How oft our prospects, seeming fair,
  Are blighted like a rose at noon,
Whose dying fragrance charms the air,
  Whose blushing petals wither soon.

E'en so our fondest hopes decay
  When to our hearts they seem secure;
And cherished friends fast pass away,
  Their virtues left as incense pure.

But faith still looks beyond the gloom
  To blest Elysian scenes outspread,
Where beauty yet again shall bloom,
  When quickened from the slumbering dead.

When unbelief would, like a cloud,
  Obscure each heavenly, blissful ray,
Which would, like blessed spirits, crowd
  Around our pathway day by day,

Then Hope lifts up the darkening veil
  That hides the welcome light above,
Whose holy influence ne'er shall fail,
  Because that light is crowned with love.

THE LAND OF THE BLEST.

How often I think of the land of the blest,
Where the pilgrim, so faint and so weary, shall rest
From his labor, his troubles, his fears, and his care,
Forever content with the peace which flows there,
Like a river abounding, unfailing, and sure,
As the words which have promised shall ever endure!
His journey so rough through this wilderness state
He now longs to end at the bright pearly gate,
Where his burden so grievous shall quickly be lost,
Which often much sorrow and anguish has cost;
Where blest angels attend on their errands of love,
E'er rejoicing to guide through the mansions above,
Oft folding their wings in their gladness to stay
To rehearse some new theme causing transport each
day;
Where sweet music celestial so charms the glad ear
As mortals ne'er dreamed in bright visions to hear;
Where the river of life, with its pure crystal sheen,
Gayly dances along with its blessings between
Those prophetical trees with their foliage so fair,
And their twelve kinds of fruit which monthly they
bear,

E'er distilling rich odors from blossom and leaf,
And a pure healthful balm for the nation's relief ;
Where pleasures unnumbered and beauties untold,
'Mid walls richly jewelled and pavements of gold,
Shall constantly burst on his wondering eyes
With the unrivalled bliss of that blest paradise.

No tears will be there ; for their fount will be dry,
And no sorrow to cause e'en one murmuring sigh ;
No long sickness to waste, and no pain to distress ;
No misfortunes to mourn, and no foes to oppress ;
No errors to grieve, nor temptations annoy ;
No sad, silent grief to diminish our joy ;
Not a long, painful day, nor a wearisome night ;
No weakness of vision, nor losing of sight ;
No privations nor losses nor evils to bear ;
Nor forebodings of ill, — the first-fruits of despair.
All, all will be tranquil and joyous and bright
In the beautified earth filled with glory and light.

There no grief shall e'er banish our pleasures away ;
No perplexing anxieties prolong their delay ;
No absence from friends, for all partings are o'er ;
No unguarded sentence in vain to deplore ;
No sin to molest our calm peace and content,
Where no chastening rod of affliction is sent ;
There envy and hatred no more can annoy,
Nor the enemy, Death, our fond hopes e'er destroy:
Then most truly that land is a land of sweet rest,
Where the weary shall find a bright home with the
blest ;

And I, as a pilgrim, now burdened, would long
With the ransomed to raise loud the conqueror's song,
Who shall triumph forever o'er death and the grave,
And bright crowns of rejoicing eternally have,
With blest angels to share in the conquest above,
And with Jesus himself in the Eden of love.

PLEASANT STREET.

The trees, denuded, shiver in the blast,
    Their honors gone, the glory of the year ;
The sky is dark and cold and overcast,
    With little *Pleasant* to afford us cheer ;
But see there, through the boughs, the church appear,
    That would not be did foliage remain ;
'Tis thus through sadness we see heaven more clear,
    And find the highest blessing through our pain.

A Grand-daughter.

VIOLETS.

EARTH so long, long dressed in ermine,
  Prized as with a royal care,
Now has changed her wintry mantle
  For her emerald robes most fair.
Lakes have oped their crystal eyelids,
  Peeping out the scene to view;
While, impatient in their bondage,
  Beauteous things have lain perdue.

Well I love the blooming spring-time,
  Coming with his sweet bequest,
— Fragrant leaves and blushing blossoms, —
  To be welcomed as a guest.
Beauty then unbidden lingers
  Round each petal, leaf, and stem,
Prized by those who see their glory
  As a bride a brilliant gem.

Then I love to wander freely,
  When the new-born light appears
Through the meads and flowery valleys,
  As in boyhood's early years.

Drinking in the balmy fragrance
  Wafted by the gentle breeze,
As an offering pure and welcome
  From the ever-whispering trees.

Wild-flowers then with joy I gather,
  With the crystal dewdrops wet,
Showing preference, and most gladly,
  To the modest violet.
Unpretending, unassuming,
  These my little pets are seen,
Quite unconscious of the glory
  Which adorns the hillocks green.

Often crushed beneath my footsteps
  When on schoolboy's rambling tour,
Even then my heart yearned kindly
  All their beauty to restore;
Now I prize them more than ever,
  Glistening in the morning ray,
On their mossy turrets posted,
  Sentinels to hail the day.

So true goodness must we cherish,
  When, unconscious of its power,
We behold a charming fragrance
  Sweet distilling hour by hour;
Blessing all with generous bounty,
  Soon reflected from above,
Leading us with grateful praises
  To the Source of purest love.

TO A FRIEND ON HER BIRTHDAY.

I KNEW a maiden young and gay,
Who used to wish her time away;
Who looked beyond those joyous hours,
Which bloom like choicest, sweetest flowers,
That scattered incense o'er life's way,
Replete with blessings day by day,
And led the bounding spirits on
To grasp new joys ere old were gone; —
Who looked beyond those sunny days,
Where no dark cloud e'er hid the rays
Of golden light, which, pure and rare,
Then gilded all things bright and fair;
When angels, borne on wings of love,
Brought peaceful tidings from above,
And whispered to the willing ear
Those pleasant tones it loved to hear,
And charmed the soul with secret peace,
Whose blessed memories never cease; —
Who looked beyond the bud of hope
For brighter prospects to spring up
(Which, if it fairer, quicker grew,
Would bear the stinging brier too),

Whose leaves, if they should chance to bloom,
Might fall as tears around its tomb, —
All fading types to plainly show
Our cherished hopes thus fade below ; —
Who looked adown the stream of life,
Whence come stern care and toil and strife,
For rarer gems of love and truth
Than those she found in early youth.

Alas ! how fast time speeds away,
With all its cares, from day to day !
With all its joys and sorrows too,
Whose cup when drained is filled anew
With mingled contents, white and red,
Of joys that live, of hopes now dead ;
Like sunshine on the mountain-cone,
We see it now, — behold, 'tis gone !
While dreary shadows show that day
Has rolled its golden car away ;
Though dews of grief should freely fall
Not one bright beam could they recall.
We gaze upon the flowing stream, —
A thing of life, no idle dream ;
Our boats are launched upon its wave,
We cannot pause, till at the grave
Our joys and hopes, our smiles and tears,
Our sad regrets, our gloomy fears,
Are buried in that boundless sea,
That endless, vast eternity.

THE SECRET WISH.

A MAIDEN sat beside a stream:
  Her face was bright and fair;
The bloom of health vied with the flowers
  Which twined her glossy hair.
Free as its crystal waters flowed
  With mellow music past,
Her joyous spirits knew that peace
  Which might not always last.

A cloud passed o'er that sunny sky,
  A shadow o'er the stream;
A secret thought possessed her breast,
  Which marred her happy dream:
"I wish I were no more a child,"
  The little maiden said,
"Nor this my home amid the flowers,
  Where fairy footsteps tread.

"I wish I were a woman fair,
  And dwelt in stately hall,
With hosts of servants ever near
  To heed my slightest call;

With wealth in rich profusion there,
To give me constant bliss,
And no more dwell in lowly cot,
'Mid rural scenes like this."

The stream still danced most gayly on,
And kissed the pebbly shore,
While lilies marked its azure track
With fragrance as before :
Around the humble doorway still
The honeysuckle grew,
Replete with fragrance, and as sweet
As Araby e'er knew.

. . . .

Years rolled away : no little feet
Now danced upon the lawn ;
No ringing laugh nor merry song
Awoke each happy dawn ;
No little hands were busy now
Among the forest bowers,
For youth with its pure joys had fled,
As incense from the flowers.

Amid the city's wearied throng,
Oppressed with toil and strife,
Where numerous ills, like dreaded foes,
Increase the cares of life ;
Where wealth itself, with all its train,
Cannot true peace supply,
I saw a being, proud and fair ;
And thus I heard her sigh : —

"My life is one of discontent,
No sunshine lights my skies:
Just when I gain some promised good,
The pleasure quickly flies.
My days are filled with bitter grief,
My cherished favorites die:
I call them back with many a tear,
But hear no kind reply.

"I long beside my native stream
Once more in peace to roam,
And drink anew those sweet delights
Which graced my happy home.
I long to hear the zephyrs pure
Soft whispering through the trees,
And feast upon rich odors borne
By every gentle breeze.

"Oh! give me back my youthful days,
— Those joyous, happy hours, —
When, free as birds upon the wing,
I roamed among the flowers.
Youth's rosy goal I since have gained,
But found both care and pain;
And now I have but one fond wish, —
Would I were young again!"

MORNING JOY.

"Weeping may endure for a night, but joy cometh in the morning."

When the dark clouds of sorrow spread over life's sky,
And no sun of gladness beams forth from on high,
Then the heart full of sadness, and heavy with grief,
Opes the fountain of tears in the hope of relief.

Though most weary and faint in our pilgrimage here,
And the rough way be wet with the oft-fallen tear,
Yet the offerings thus given shall not be in vain,
But as pearls of rejoicing be numbered again.

The fairest of flowers in silence may bloom,
And in secret distribute the richest perfume ;
Even so, when afflictions our chalice may fill,
Then the sweetest of comforts for us may distil.

Brightest gems often lie where no footsteps may go,
Which need but the light all their value to show ;
And those spots which the valley of tears often seem
Are the mountains of peace seen in rapturous dream.

Like a stranger benighted in darkness most drear,
Where no kind word is heard, and no bright stars
appear,
The soul in its weariness pines for the day
Which shall banish the shadows that obscured his
lone way.

Though the night may be long, and trials and woes
Oft encompass our path, and disturb our repose,
A blest morn shall soon dawn, when ineffable joy
Shall insure that true peace which no time can destroy.

The glorious light of that heavenly day,
Which shall burst on our sight with its unfading ray,
Shall reveal in its splendor the proofs of that love
Which has guided our feet while we journeyed above.

Though the hand be unseen which shall glide through
the gloom,
And no voices be heard as we march to the tomb,
Yet we know that His presence is near to defend
Who has promised forever His flock to attend.

When the night shall be past, and immortal we stand
By the river of life in that beautiful land,
We shall find that those trials which caused our delay
Were but angels of mercy encamped by the way.

Still confiding, still trusting, and knowing no fear,
We will cling to those hopes we have ever held dear,
Till the morning shall break, and the sun shall arise
On the mansions prepared for the just in the skies.

THE ROSE BY THE WAYSIDE.

A LITTLE rose bloomed in the way
O'er which I roamed one sunny day:
It looked so fair,
I wondered why alone it grew,
And why so long concealed from view,
While nestling there.

Its crimson petals wide outspread
A grateful perfume freely shed;
Dripping with dew,
It seemed in whispered tones to say,
"Shunning the glances of the gay,
I bloomed for you.

"The sunshine kissed my petals gay,
Soon as I peeped to hail the day,
With blushes red;
I was content, though hid from view:
No other footsteps this way drew,
By beauty led."

I claimed the treasure, pure and fair,
As all mine own: with special care
    I kept it long:
It said sweet sayings o'er and o'er;
But one bright morn it spoke no more, —
    Its leaves were gone.

Thus in the varied paths of life,
Amid its cares, its toils, its strife,
    We often roam:
Then some sweet memories chain us here,
Some holy thoughts dispel all fear,
    And guide us home.

And when earth's charms, like withered flowers,
Amid afflictions painful hours,
    No longer cheer,
A holy peace, a quiet joy,
Which unbelief can ne'er destroy,
    Brings heaven near.

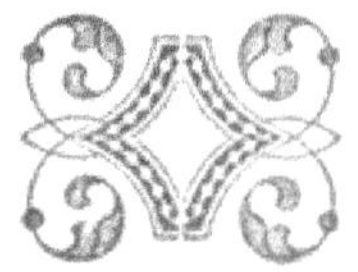

A MORNING WALK.

WHEN the sun is brightly beaming
In the morning sky,
And, awaking from their dreaming,
Wild-flowers look on high,
Violets blue,
All wet with dew,
Bid our roaming footsteps linger,
As each points with jewelled finger
To the azure clouds, which seem
Fairy-lands of which they dream.

Birdlings with their bosoms yearning
For the days of spring,
To their summer homes returning,
From the south-land bring
Melodies sweet,
With love replete,
Leading our best thoughts to heaven,
As sweet incense gladly given
To that God who guards us all,
Watching e'en the sparrow's fall.

Flowerets in the woodland breathing
Silent words of prayer,
To the passing breeze bequeathing
Fragrance pure and rare,
Bring to us joy
Without alloy,
As with pleasure we bend o'er them,
Humbly worshipping before them,
Reading on each petal fair
Precious truths abiding there.

Music from pure fountains gushing,
Sparkling clear and free,
O'er the pebbly pavements rushing,
Toward the deep-blue sea,
Falls on my ear,
Listening to hear,
As in days of happy childhood,
When I roamed far in the wildwood,
Gathering lilies from the brooks,
Floating in fair shady nooks.

Thus in Memory's halls I wander
Where I used to tread,
And in silence often ponder
On scenes long, long fled,
Wishing to view
Sunshine and dew,
On some bright and lovely morning,
When sweet flowers, the meads adorning,
Breathe sweet odors on the air,
Giving blessing everywhere.

Near "still waters" soon forever
Joyous feet shall stand,
Where earth's fairest scenes shall never
Fade in that blest land;
Where'er for thee
Glory shall be,
On the blooming plains of Eden,
'Neath the brilliant skies of heaven,
Untold bliss awaits each soul,
Sighing for that shining goal.

TIME'S CHANGES

TIME is flitting fast away,
And must close life's changeful day:
Morning clouds all tinged with red,
Find at eve their curtained bed,
Where, in sighs and tears forlorn,
Mourn they glories of the morn.

Pleasures here may bloom a while,
And our saddest thoughts beguile,
Yielding up their treasures rare
To delight life's morning air;
But their province soon must close,
Like the clouds, in night's repose.

Stars may sparkle bright on high
Gemming all the midnight sky,
Soothing thoughts all quiet bringing,
Unknown vespers silent singing;
Yet must fail their gentle ray
Quickly at the rising day;

So earth's scenes may brightly glare,
Tempting with their winning air,
'Mid the gloom their light revealing,
Purer treasures often stealing,
Showing oft their secret power
False, when comes life's evening hour,
Causing oft the midnight tear,
Secret falling, none to hear,
Perishing like stars of night
Soon before a holier light.

All is changing here below:
Earth's delights, — a fleeting show;
Flowers bloom to droop and fade
On green lawn, in valley's shade;
Winds a mournful requiem sing;
Bursting clouds their tribute bring;
Beauty reigns, too soon it dies,
Though passing sweet its mysteries;
Friends are found who love and bless,
Death soon makes the number less;
All is changing like the sea;
Pleasures come, as quickly flee,
Perishing, to stay no more
Than the bubbles on the shore.

But upon the shining shore
Beauty lives to die no more;
Flowers bloom in brighter dress,
Glorious with their loveliness;
Friendship's bonds no grief will sever,
Pain and tears be lost forever,

Music linger on the ear,
In such notes as angels hear,
Glory from the throne above
Filling all with peace and love ;
All are happy, all are blest,
In that blissful world of rest.

THE LITTLE FAVORITE.

My favorite was a charming pet
  But just four summers old;
Her merry laugh is ringing yet,
  Her worth was never told.
A lily rested on her brow,
  A rose upon her cheek;
But, though as pure as spotless snow,
  Death came the flower to seek.

Her eyes were of a heavenly blue,
  So bright, so soft, so fair,
That thoughts within her heart so true
  Were read most quickly there.
Rich clustering curls, where golden light
  Had found a dwelling-place,
Hung o'er her dimpled shoulders white
  With most bewitching grace.

The presence of this fairy bright
  Brought sunshine home to all;
The echo of her footsteps light
  Was music in the hall.

I left "my little rosebud" fair
  At play with other flowers,
And hoped no cloud of sadness there
  Would shade life's purest hours.

I saw the darling as she lay
  Upon her bed of pain,
And wore the weary hours away,
  Inviting sleep again.
I saw the signet on her brow,
  Of one who knew his own:
Her friends were weeping sadly now,
  Nor mourned they quite alone.

. . . . .

'Twas twilight hour; the room was still,
  And smooth her little bed:
A cloud of sombre gloom and chill
  O'er all things seemed to spread.
While gazing round, the truth was shown
  In toys and vacant chair,—
An angel from that home had flown
  That had abided there.

Her little hands upon her breast
  In peaceful quiet lay,
As if she thus had sunk to rest
  Upon a summer day.
The smile upon her face was seen,
  Which she was wont to wear;
As if she thus in dreams serene
  Found pleasure everywhere.

An angel bright had kindly come
  Adown the starry skies
To guide her to that glorious home
  Where beauty never dies.
She knew the blest one when he came,
  With shining garments white;
For she before had seen the same
  In vision of the night.

But in life's mingled cup is known
  A precious, heavenly balm,
Which, when the heart is sad and lone,
  With soothing power can charm;
Blest sunshine then, through cheerless gloom,
  Reveals a brighter day,
And faith beholds beyond the tomb
  That home where angels stay.

YES, THEN I'LL THINK OF YOU.

When morn with rosy beams is seen
  To kiss the dew from leaf and flower,
And bid the tinted roses spread
  Their petals fair to grace the bower,
Then, when I see each lovely hue, —
Yes, then, my friend, I'll think of you.

When night with sombre curtain hides
  The golden beams of life and light,
When sparkling gems attract our eyes
  With brilliant rays, like diamonds bright,
When first thy favorite star I view, —
Yes, then, my friend, I'll think of you.

When springtime comes, all gay and bright,
  Rejoicing in its new-born life,
When songsters tune their little throats
  To strains unknown to mortal strife,
When earth is dressed in robes most new, —
Yes, then, my friend, I'll think of you.

When scenes of pleasure cheer my heart,
  And tranquil thoughts afford delight,
When beauteous prospects, decked with flowers,
  Can charm the mind and please the sight,
Where'er such lovely scenes I view,
Yes, then, my friend, I'll think of you.

When in retirement memory steals
  To happy days, forever past;
When every hour new joys increased,
  Too sweet were they to longer last, —
Yes, then, when friends their pledge renew,
I love to think, my friend, of you.

When lonely hours, all filled with gloom,
  Exert their power to grieve the mind;
When, if one voice I then should hear,
  A source of peace I soon should find;
When kindred hearts are far and few,
Then most, my friend, I'll think of you.

A SILENT TOKEN.

THIS friendly sign
I soon divine,
Though not a smile be seen,
Or kindly word
In darkness heard
At twilight hour serene.

'Tis sunshine bright,
Of mellow light,
Which shines amid the gloom,
And warms the heart
With magic art,
Nor fades in airs of doom.

E'en as the dew,
Of rainbow hue,
Soft nestles in a flower,
On two lips fair,
It resteth there
As in a perfumed bower.

'Tis nectar sweet,
With love replete,
Which charms the passing hours,
Where sweet thoughts stay,
Like bees in May,
Around the fragrant flowers.

It seals the word
Which love has heard
With sympathy sincere,
And sweetens care,
Though pains be there,
Or many a falling tear.

Still let me know
The bliss below
Which loving souls can feel;
And in sweet dreams
Let sunny beams
O'er my glad spirits steal.

TO GAROPHELIA.

THOUGH pure and holy be the bond
Which holds us by its tenure fond,
And bids us twine a sacred bower
In token of each pleasant hour,
Yet have we here no emblems fair,
With which our cherished thoughts to share.

But in affection's shrine will be
Enduring gems of constancy,
Which will reflect both joy and peace
When cold deceit and flattery cease,
And shed a lustre o'er our way,
With sweet content, from day to day.

True friendship sheds a holy light
In gloomy sorrow's dismal night,
And studs its curtain, dark and drear,
With stars — pure kindly acts — most dear
To suffering ones, oppressed with care,
Who oft no tender feelings share.

Our happiest moments, pure, serene,
Brighten like flowers a dreary scene;
And like their fragrance may convey
Sweet solace in a darksome day.
They calmly cheer the ills of earth,
Where gloom, with its sad train, has birth.

Yet in fond memory shall abide
Each friendly act, whate'er betide;
Each pleasing wish, all proffered aid,
Shall still remain when health shall fade,
With kindly influence e'er to cheer
A lonely heart when pains are near.

ANOTHER YEAR.

WHAT joys and hopes, what griefs and fears,
Are numbered with the fleeting years!
What trials crowd the path of life!
What grievous cares, what busy strife!
What tears bedew the brightest eye!
What shadows veil the sunniest sky!
What teeming thoughts, with joy attune,
Are born, alas! to die too soon!

As Time's swift chariot rolls along,
Filled with its vast and varied throng,
All eager for that shining goal
Which can appease the longing soul;
How very few, alas! can tell
Of secret peace which charmeth well,
Or speak of hopes, by faith made sure,
As living truths which must endure.

How many a joyous heart has seen
Bright prospects fail, as, in a dream,
One sees some cherished object fly
Just when it seemed approaching nigh!

How many a sunny spot, once fair,
Now feels the blight of sorrow there,
Because its loveliest flower has fled,
No more to grace its native bed!

The purest and the best depart,
And leave a gloom within the heart,
Dispelled alone but by that power
Which can illume the darkest hour.
Then sweetest memories gather fast
Around the sainted of the past,
Which bid us still unwearied view
The pearly gate they entered through.

Another year has rolled away,
Another year has dawned to-day,
Bright with the hopes of joy and peace,
And crowned with gifts rich with increase.
May purest blessings from above,
Distilling from the Fount of Love,
Fill every heart, both rich and poor,
So that no soul could ask for more!

And as the seasons pass away
Which nearer bring the perfect day,
Which knows no pain nor toil nor care,
Nor shadows dark, nor trials there,
Should we be called to that sweet rest,
Which e'er awaits the truly blest,
May we with joy the summons hear,
And triumph over every fear!

NEARER HOME.

WHY should I fear the ocean's foam?
Its waves but bear me nearer home:
Though stormy winds my bark assail,
She still outrides the boisterous gale,
And, bounding on her homeward way,
She nears the harbor day by day;
And soon her sails will all be furled
Close by the shores of the better world.
  Oh, that beautiful world!

Dark billows long my bark have tost;
Life's dearest hopes have all been lost;
Shut from the heritage of light,
My days are changed to gloomy night.
Though in a foreign land I roam,
My longing heart still sighs for home,
And still I seek the heavenly shore,
Where waves of trouble flow no more.
  Oh, that beautiful world!

Afflictions are the storms which bear
Our trembling barks more swiftly there,
And pains and tears the boiling foam
Which speeds us quicker, nearer home;

While faith and hope beam o'er the way,
And angel forms around us stay
To guard us till life's ills be past,
And guide us to the port at last.
 Oh, that beautiful world!

Then bear me on, nor let me fear,
Though untried storms may yet be near;
Let me but hear my Father's voice,
Then his blest will shall be my choice,
Till in the realms of bliss I prove
His constant, never-failing love,
Who leads me by his own right hand
Into the holy promised land.
 Oh, that beautiful world!

Then courage, soul, and ne'er despond!
Behold the glorious scene beyond,
Where loved ones who have gone before
Shall greet us on the heavenly shore;
Where tears shall all be wiped away,
And darkness changed to perfect day;
Where songs of triumph e'er shall swell
The praises of Immanuël.
 Oh, that beautiful world!

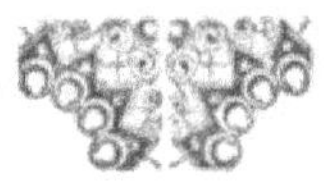

LET ME REST.

LET me rest soon in peace: I am weary of earth,
Where tears have their fountain, and sorrows have birth;
Let me cease from my labors, and find that repose
Which in heaven the earth-wearied soul only knows.

Let me rest from all trouble; for pain is my lot,
Since darkness has clouded life's sunniest spot.
In vain do bright flowers blush kindly for me;
For their beautiful petals I never may see.

Let me rest from all trial, all sadness and sin,
To endless felicity soon enter in,
To enjoy then forever with purest delight
Those wonders which now are withholden my sight.

Let the friends, as they come to my cold, silent bier,
Leave a flower, but bring not a sigh nor a tear;
Let them keep in fond memory my poor, humble name, —
Not lost to affection, though dead to earth's fame.

I wish to be laid, in my last, silent sleep,
Where in quiet repose dewy violets weep
Their diamond tears on each fair summer's morn,
As a tribute of love my lone grave to adorn.

Let birds fearless come to my emerald bed,
And joyously sport o'er the slumbering dead;
Let them shatter the silence with jubilant song,
As echoes borne earthward from heaven's glad throng.

Let sunshine play o'er me through tall, waving trees,
Let anthems be sung by the murmuring breeze,
Let nature around me look happy and gay,
To drive every vestige of gloom far away.

I would leave such a blessing of sanctified peace
As would savor of heaven and bid sorrow cease;
I'd smooth the rough pathway of those left below,
And life's sweetest gifts on them ever bestow.

www.ingramcontent.com/pod-product-compliance
Lightning Source LLC
Chambersburg PA
CBHW030347270326
41926CB00009B/988

9783337004989